COUNTING
YOUR
CALORIES

———

COUNTING YOUR CALORIES

Dr Patricia Judd &
Dr Gabi Reaidi

CHANCELLOR
PRESS

First published as *Hamlyn Help Yourself Guide: Counting Your Calories* in 1989 by Reed Consumer Books Limited

This edition published in 1993 by Chancellor Press
an imprint of Reed Consumer Books Limited
Michelin House, 81 Fulham Road, London SW3 6RB
and Auckland, Melbourne, Singapore and Toronto

ISBN 1 85152 367 7

A CIP catalogue record for this book is available from
the British Library

Printed in Great Britain

CONTENTS

INTRODUCTION

Calorie counting can help you plan your diet in an enjoyable way so as to attain and maintain your ideal weight. Be sensible, however, about trying to reduce weight. Crash diets can result in dramatic weight loss but will *never* help you stay slim. A poorly planned or badly balanced diet consisting of a pattern of over-eating followed by starvation means you will end up feeling lethargic and unhealthy because your body rhythms are upset.

Remember proper all-round nourishment comes from a variety of foods to supply the basic nutrients (proteins, fats and carbohydrates), together with the vitamins and minerals they contain, which go to make up a healthy diet. So it is important for all of them, in varying quantities, to feature in your diet. Understanding how these different foods affect your metabolism will enable you to develop a Calorie controlled diet that will help you to lose weight and is also appetizing and nutritious.

WHAT ARE CALORIES (AND KILOJOULES)?

The energy used up in activity and taken in as food is measured in kilocalories, more often just called Calories. Nowadays, under the modern system, the term kilojoules is also used. One Calorie equals approximately 4.2 kilojoules so if you want to convert kilojoules into Calories (for example if you find energy given in kilojoules but not Calories on some packaged foods) simply divide the number of kilojoules by 4.2.

THE ESSENTIAL NUTRIENTS IN

PROTEINS

Proteins are essential, body-building materials found in meat, fish, milk, cheese and eggs. Pulses – dried beans, peas and lentils – are rich in protein, and smaller amounts are contained in many other foods such as bread and potatoes. Even if you cut down on the protein foods it is important that you should not omit them entirely from your diet.

An adult needs to obtain 10 per cent of his or her energy as protein each day. Therefore, on a 2000 Calorie diet, 200 Calories should be protein and, as protein supplies 4 Calories per gram, the total weight of protein intake per day will be 50 grams (1⅔ oz). From the table you can see that you could get all you need each day from half a pint of milk, 180 grams (6 oz) of meat and 4 slices of bread.

High Protein Foods	
Food	*Grams of Protein per 30 grams (1 oz)*
Fish	3-7
Meat	5-7
Cheese	4-8
Milk	1
Pulse vegetables (dry)	5-8
Bread	2-3
Potatoes	0.4-1
Egg (1 only)	6

CARBOHYDRATES

These are the starches and sugars which make up about half of most people's diet. Their main function in the body is as an energy supply. Sugar is the most concentrated and purest carbohydrate and provides no other nutrients – it's just a source of energy. This applies to brown and white sugar and for this reason these foods are said to contain 'empty Calories', as are things like sweets and fizzy drinks. Sugars are also found in less concentrated form in all fruits, which are more importantly a useful source of vitamins and fibre (see below). If you are trying to cut down on carbohydrates and sugar you should still include some (unsweetened, if cooked or canned) fruit in your diet.

The other carbohydrate-containing foods are cereals, e.g. break-fast cereals, or flour, bread, pasta, and root vegetables such as potatoes which also contain starch. Cereals and root vegetables or 'starchy carbohydrates' contain other essential nutrients as well. This group of carbohydrates, therefore, is an important part of a healthy diet, though not when combined with large amounts of sugar or fat.

FIBRE

Starchy carbohydrates also contain dietary fibre which plays an important part in a healthy diet as it stimulates and helps the digestive system. Foods that are high in fibre also help give a feeling of fullness even though they are often low in Calories and so can be helpful in a slimming diet. Pulses, as well as fruit and vegetables, are a useful source of fibre if you are on a diet which cuts down on cereals and potatoes.

FATS

The main sources of fat in the diet are butter, margarine, other cooking fats and oils and, less obviously, dairy products and meat. Even in very lean meat there is still a certain amount of hidden fat and similarly, oily fish like salmon or herring also have a high fat content. Other sources are cakes, biscuits and pastries.

In western countries we eat more fat than we need because fats make foods taste pleasant. In many foods the particular flavour we associate with that food is in the fat. We really only need to get about 10 per cent of our energy from fat in order to satisfy the body's requirements. Most people eat much more than this.

Fats are a very concentrated energy source – for this reason anyone on a slimming diet should be careful to avoid too many high fat foods.

Help yourself avoid an excess of fat in your diet by cutting down on butter and margarine and using a low-fat spread instead. (These have half as many Calories as butter or ordinary margarine.) Remember that other dairy products such as milk, cream and many kinds of cheese also have a high fat content; get round this by using skimmed milk or skimmed milk powder, yoghurt instead of cream, and low-fat cottage cheese rather than full-fat soft cheese. There are also new low-fat hard cheeses available – so try these instead of cheddar and other cholesterol-high types.

Finally, adapt your cooking techniques to help control your fat intake too: trim all excess fat from meat and grill rather than fry. Make it a rule to cut right down on fried foods, but when frying is essential, always use a non-stick pan, with which a minimum of fat is needed. You can also drain fried food on kitchen towel to soak up extra fat before serving.

MINERAL SALTS

Several minerals are important for the healthy functioning of the body. These include sodium (as salt), potassium, magnesium, phosphate and others such as copper, iodine and zinc, which are only needed in very small amounts. If we eat a varied diet it is unlikely that we would go short of any of these.

Two minerals which are needed in larger amounts, and which can sometimes be low in the diet of people trying to slim, are:

CALCIUM

This is needed to build and maintain strong bones and teeth. Adults need about half a gram a day, children twice as much. This is usually obtained from milk, cheese and other dairy products in this country, although bread, to which calcium is added, is also a useful source. Other sources are canned fish, such as salmon and sardines, where the bones are eaten, and green vegetables.

IRON

This is needed for the red pigment in the blood, which carries oxygen to all the tissues. If there is insufficient iron in the diet, anaemia may result. This is not uncommon, especially in women, who lose iron in the menstrual blood loss.

Iron is found in meat (particularly offal such as liver and kidneys) and is easily absorbed from these animal foods. The iron in other foods is less well absorbed, so cereals and green vegetables may look good on paper but aren't so good in practice. Eggs used to be regarded as a good source of iron, but it's now recognized that the iron is poorly absorbed and may even lower the absorption of iron from other foods eaten with them.

VITAMINS

There are thirteen different vitamins known to be important for a healthy body; they are chemically very different and without them the system cannot make use of the other essential nutrients. Some vitamins are associated with fat in foods and others with the non-fat part. These are called fat-soluble and water-soluble respectively. Fat-soluble vitamins are stored in the body and can be harmful in excess; surplus water-soluble vitamins are excreted, therefore they are harmless although excessive amounts are still best avoided.

FAT SOLUBLE VITAMINS

Vitamin	Function	Sources
A	Helps keep mucous membranes healthy. Essential for vision in dim light.	Dairy products; eggs; enriched margarine; cod liver oil. Also made from carotene in green plants and carrots.
D	Necessary for formation of healthy bones.	Cod liver oil; fatty fish e.g. herrings, kippers; dairy produce; enriched margarine. Also formed by the action of sunlight on skin.
E	Function not fully understood.	Cereals, especially wholemeal; eggs; butter; green leafy vegetables.
K	Essential for blood clotting.	Green leafy vegetables; fruits; nuts; wholegrain cereals.

WATER-SOLUBLE VITAMINS

	Function	Sources
B_1	Helps release energy from foods and makes best use of protein.	Wholegrain cereals; legumes; meat, especially pork and bacon, liver and kidneys; yeast extract; flour.

B_2	As B_1	Milk; meat; liver; eggs; cheese; green leafy vegetables; yeast extract.
Nicotinic Acid	As B_1	Wholegrain cereals; pulses; meat, especially liver; fortified breakfast cereals.
Biotin	As B_1	Yeast; nuts; liver and kidney; green vegetables.
C	Important for healing and generally maintaining tissues.	Fruit, especially citrus; green vegetables; tomatoes; potatoes.
Folic Acid	For formation of all cells in the body, for blood formation.	Liver; pulses; wholegrain cereals; green vegetables.
B_6	General metabolism.	Meat; vegetables; yeast; wholegrain cereals.
B_{12}	Formation of new cells especially blood.	Meat, especially liver; dairy products. Absent from plants.
Pantothenic Acid	Used in metabolism.	All foods.

ARE YOU OVERWEIGHT?

If you are reading this book the chances are that you are worried about your weight. But it is important to be aware that it is really excess fat which matters, not weight itself. Some people have a heavier build than others and athletes who develop large muscles may be above the ideal range of weight even though they are not fat. The charts on page 13 are simplified versions of the ideal weight tables used by insurance companies. They show a range of weights for each height. The 'suitable' weight range is based on the average ideal weight for the different frame sizes. An honest glance in the mirror will often tell you what you want to know – and use your common sense in deciding whether dieting is the best approach to take. You may find that increasing your muscle tone a bit will do more for your shape than starving off additional inches! After all, a bit of exercise to keep your figure in trim is a far healthier approach than living permanently on a restricted diet.

WHY DO SOME PEOPLE START TO GAIN WEIGHT?

Gaining weight usually happens either because you have been taking in more energy (Calories) in your food than you have been using up *or* because you have been eating the same amount as you were when your weight was lower, but are becoming less active.

There seem to be several danger points at which people gain weight – many people say they started to gain weight when they got married; for some women pregnancy is the time when they gain weight and they don't lose it after their babies are born. Gaining weight because of using less energy is common in people who are getting older – the so-called middle-aged spread. This doesn't necessarily happen as you get older, though there is some evidence that the metabolic rate slows down a little with age and this will tend to make weight gain more likely. Any change in lifestyle which means cutting down on the amount of exercise you do may let the weight creep on. And, of course, extra weight can become a disincentive to take exercise . . .

HOW CAN YOU TAKE OFF WEIGHT?

In order to lose weight you have to take in less energy than you need for your level of activity, so that you will use up the store of fat to produce energy and will gradually get thinner. It may seem that there are two ways of doing this – either by cutting down on food or by increasing the amount of energy you use up.

Exercise can help prevent weight gain and may have some effect on the way the body burns up energy. Calorie for Calorie, however, you have to increase your activity by a large amount in order to make much difference to your weight. For example, the average

Weight Ranges – Men

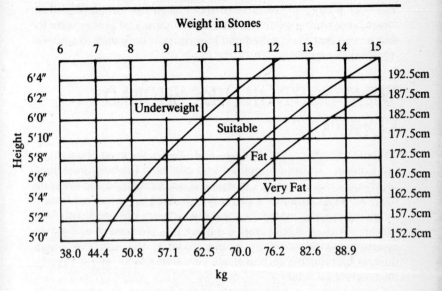

Weight Ranges – Women

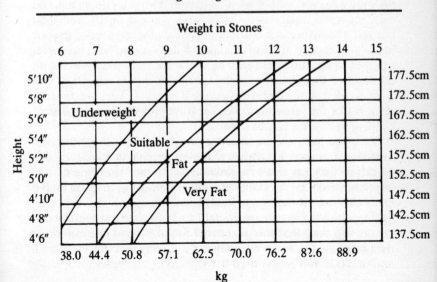

person would have to walk about 160 kilometres (100 miles) to lose just over 1 kg (2 lb) of fat. For this reason few people find that increasing exercise alone will take off weight as fast as they want to lose it, and that a controlled diet is essential if they want to achieve significant weight loss.

WHAT SORT OF DIET SHOULD I CHOOSE?

There are many types of diet available. Two of the most popular are the Calorie Controlled method and the Low Carbohydrate diet described here. Counting Calories is the basic method and many of the other diets around are just ways of taking the effort out of this by giving specific menus or meals, which are designed with low Calorie foods. Carbohydrate counting is a refinement of Calorie counting, which works by cutting down Calories in two ways: directly by reducing carbohydrate-containing foods and indirectly by lowering fat intake.

One way you can help yourself to decide which diet is suitable is to keep a record of everything you eat for a few days. Write down not only what you eat but when, where and why. By doing this you may get some insight into the reasons you eat, apart from real hunger. Then you can see what changes, if any, are needed in your life to help cope with being on a diet. A daily record will also reveal whether you normally eat a lot or a little and help you to decide on the level of Calories or carbohydrates you should eat. Once you have decided on the diet there's no real benefit in keeping constant records like this; they may even substitute for the real business of keeping to the diet you have chosen.

Once you have chosen your diet work out a meal pattern that suits you. Research has shown that many people lose weight more quickly if they eat small frequent meals, rather than one or two large ones each day, as eating little and often seems to speed up the metabolic rate. If this is not possible compromise by having three light meals each day with small snacks in between. You use up more energy digesting that way and avoid the likelihood of bingeing at the end of the day when your activity is usually at its lowest. You'll also find that you're less tired in the evening as a result.

14

WHICH DIET SUITS YOU?

The Calorie Controlled plan is useful:
- if you only have a little weight to lose.
- if you don't mind weighing and measuring foods and keeping a running total of the Calories you've eaten.
- if you find it difficult to resist sweet and starchy foods.
- if you tend to nibble between meals.
- if you've already lost some weight by another method but seem to be stuck.

The Low Carbohydrate diet is useful:
- if you are prepared to do some weighing and measuring but not to devote a lot of effort to this.
- if you have a family to cook for or eat out often with friends or in restaurants.
- if you have a lot of weight to lose or you have never tried to diet before.
- if you feel you can cut out sweet and starchy foods and alcohol without feeling deprived.
- if you are not tempted to nibble.

THE CALORIE CONTROLLED METHOD

First you must decide on your Calorie intake. You can do this by working out your energy requirements and cutting your intake below this level or by working out the Calorie content of what you are eating at the moment and cutting down on that. Either way the Calorie level chosen, in practice, is usually between 1000 and 1500 Calories per day.

1500 Calories are suitable if:
- you are physically very active, so your energy needs are high (e.g. an athlete, or a mother with active young children).
- you are used to eating large meals and would find it difficult to keep to 1000 Calories.
- you have more than 12 kg (2 stones) to lose. It is better to start with a higher limit as it will be easier to keep to over the period required to attain this weight loss.

1000 Calories are suitable if:
(a) you don't eat much at the moment.
(b) you are not very active (e.g. a desk worker).
(c) you have less than 12 kg (2 stone) to lose.

As long as you are eating fewer Calories than you are using up you will lose weight. The important thing is to choose a level which you can keep to. If you set it too low it's unlikely you'd be able to keep to it long enough for it to be effective.

It is not advisable to go below 1000 Calories without medical supervision, though of course that doesn't mean you can't go below that level occasionally. You may find that you want to save some Calories for a special meal or celebration. Similarly, your Calorie intake may be unevenly spread over the week; an irregular count, provided it averages out, may suit a lifestyle where weekends involve 'social' eating.

HOW TO MANAGE THE DIET

Remember, it is important to maintain a nutritionally healthy diet. You would lose weight if you took all your 1000 Calories as chocolate cake or cream buns, but this wouldn't be good for your health or complexion!

Select a sensible variety of foods within the Calorie limit you set yourself. A good general rule is to keep about half your Calorie allowance for foods which are high in essential nutrients, such as meat, fish, eggs, green vegetables and fruit. In practice this means avoiding high fat foods as these have most Calories and to some extent avoiding high carbohydrate foods.

To start with, it is useful to weigh foods in order to calculate the Calorie value of your meals with reasonable accuracy as it is difficult to estimate the weight of portions when you aren't used to it. After a while you will get used to the size of portions and it will be enough just to check occasionally to ensure you aren't under-estimating the size, especially if you stop losing weight.

THE LOW CARBOHYDRATE DIET

This diet, devised by Professor John Yudkin, relies on cutting sugary and starchy foods to a minimum. It is therefore slightly

Energy/Activity Chart

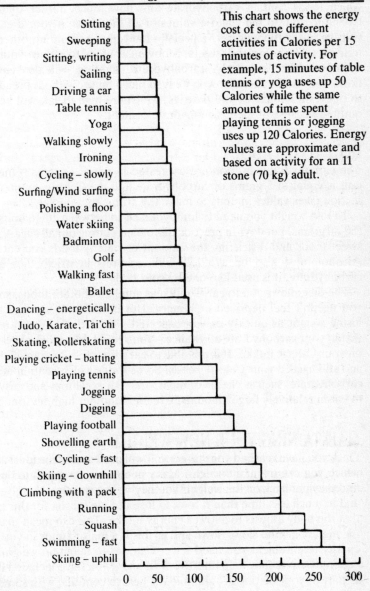

This chart shows the energy cost of some different activities in Calories per 15 minutes of activity. For example, 15 minutes of table tennis or yoga uses up 50 Calories while the same amount of time spent playing tennis or jogging uses up 120 Calories. Energy values are approximate and based on activity for an 11 stone (70 kg) adult.

Sitting
Sweeping
Sitting, writing
Sailing
Driving a car
Table tennis
Yoga
Walking slowly
Ironing
Cycling – slowly
Surfing/Wind surfing
Polishing a floor
Water skiing
Badminton
Golf
Walking fast
Ballet
Dancing – energetically
Judo, Karate, Tai'chi
Skating, Rollerskating
Playing cricket – batting
Playing tennis
Jogging
Digging
Playing football
Shovelling earth
Cycling – fast
Skiing – downhill
Climbing with a pack
Running
Squash
Swimming – fast
Skiing – uphill

0   50   100   150   200   250   300

simpler than the Calorie counting method: you only need to know which foods contain carbohydrate and how much, rather than having to add up the Calorie values of all the items in your diet. Cutting out carbohydrates, especially foods that contain no other nutrients, like sugar and sweets, is obviously going to reduce your Calorie intake. Indirectly, carbohydrate counting will also cut down your fat intake: you won't eat so much butter without bread to put it on and cakes and pastries, which are high in fat, will be omitted because of their carbohydrate content.

HOW TO GO ABOUT IT

The carbohydrates in food are expressed in grams or units. One unit is equal to 5 grams of carbohydrate and the Calorie counter section gives values in units to make the arithmetic simpler.

To lose weight you need to limit yourself to between 10-16 units (50-80 grams) per day. In practice this means cutting out all sugary, sweet foods and restricting the amount of starchy foods you eat. Alcohol must also be avoided; although this is strictly not a carbohydrate, it is used like one by your body.

The diet allows you to eat as much as you like of other foods, so you needn't feel deprived or hungry. But if you find you aren't losing weight as quickly as you expected – even though you are within your carbohydrate allowance – you should do a quick check on your Calorie intake. It is possible to eat a low carbohydrate diet and still exceed your Calorie needs. Some foods which contain no carbohydrate, such as cheese or meat, are high in calories and easy to eat in relatively large amounts. Cream is another high fat food.

MAINTAINING YOUR NEW WEIGHT

Once you have reached your target you will need to find the level at which you can maintain weight. Many people are disappointed to find they put back on the weight that they've lost so painstakingly – and in much less time than it took to lose it. One reason for this is that the body adjusts to a lower energy intake. This can mean that the metabolic rate slows down and as this is a major factor in your energy requirement you need fewer Calories to maintain weight. Again, exercise may help improve this, and if you have included it as part of your dieting programme it's best to continue with some form of exercise afterwards.

To find your new level of food intake you'll need to check your weight once a week and gradually increase your intake. Suppose you lost weight by Calorie counting. Try eating an extra 200 Calories the first week, and then an extra 100 or 200 Calories each week until you find the level at which you start to gain weight again. Then go back one or two steps and stay at that level.

If you've been losing weight using the low-carbohydrate method, you can increase your energy intake by either of two ways (or a mixture of both). You may have got used to doing without sugary and starchy foods and may find it easier to do without them completely rather than have a small amount. In that case you could increase your intake of carbohydrate free foods.

Alternatively, you might want to have more bread and potatoes – in that case increase your carbohydrate units e.g. from 10 to 15 or from 16 to 20. It's best not to do it all at once though as your body will store the excess carbohydrate along with some water and your weight may shoot up rapidly. As with Calorie counting find a level at which your weight is steady and don't let the weight go up by more than 1 or 2 kg (2-4 lb). If you find this is happening, go back to your diet until you get it under control.

USING THE CALORIE COUNTER

The values given in the following table cannot be regarded as absolute values for any food item you eat. The only way to find the real value of all food would be to chemically analyse it. However, they are accurate enough for you to control your Calorie or carbohydrate intake.

The Calories and carbohydrate units are given per oz (30 grams) and per portion. The portion size is described in the final column. In some cases the portion size is left as 1 oz (30 g), e.g. for raw weights when the food would be weighed before cooking.

All Calorie values have been rounded up or down to the nearest 5 Calories, thus some of the figures for the portions are not direct multiples of those given for 1 oz (30 g). The exception is values below 5 Calories per oz where the nearest whole number is given.

Carbohydrate units are expressed to the nearest ¼ of a 5 g unit for low values; to the nearest ½ for high carbohydrate foods.

THE

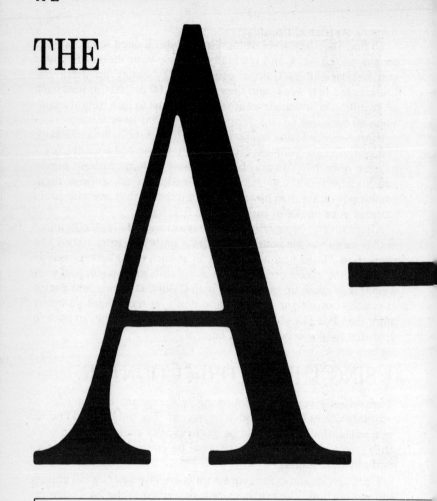

The calculations for the tables have been worked out using ounces as the standard measure. Metric equivalents have been given in brackets. They are exact conversions (1 oz × 28.4 g) rounded up to whole grams, except that the 1 oz portions have been rounded up to 30 g for convenience. As kitchen scales are not so accurate when you are measuring you will find it easier to

TABLES

round up or down to the nearest 5 grams so if for example you are weighing 57 g of cooked dahl, 55 g is the amount to aim for; whereas with 114 g of roast forerib you would measure 115 g.

No distinction has been made for fluid ounces, they are treated the same as ounces.

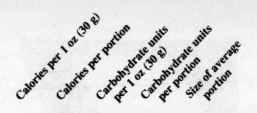

	Calories per 1 oz (30 g)	Calories per portion	Carbohydrate units per 1 oz (30 g)	Carbohydrate units per portion	Size of average portion
Abalone					
raw	30	30	0	0	1 oz (30 g)
steamed	25	125	0	0	5 oz (142 g)
canned	25	125	0	0	5 oz (142 g)
fried	35	175	0	0	5 oz (142 g)
ackee, canned	45	180	0	0	4 oz (114 g)
advocaat	75	75	3	3	1 oz (30 g)

ALCOHOLIC DRINKS

ale					
brown, bottled	10	100	½	3	½ pt (284 ml)
pale, bottled	10	100	½	5	½ pt (284 ml)
strong	20	200	1	10	½ pt (284 ml)
anisette	65	65	3	3	1 oz (30 ml)
armagnac	65	65	3	3	1 oz (30 ml)
barley wine	20	200	1	10	½ pt (284 ml)

	Calories per 1 oz (30 g)	Calories per portion	Carbohydrate units per 1 oz (30 g)	Carbohydrate units per portion	Size of average portion
beer					
canned, bitter	10	100	½	5	½ pt (284 ml)
draught, bitter	10	100	½	5	½ pt (284 ml)
draught, mild	5	50	¼	3	½ pt (284 ml)
benedictine	110	110	5	5	1 oz (30 ml)
blackcurrant liqueur	70	70	3	3	1 oz (30 ml)
Bloody Mary	30	210	1¼	9	7 oz (199 ml)
bourbon	65	65	3	3	1 oz (30 ml)
calvados	70	70	3	3	1 oz (30 ml)
cassis	70	70	3	3	1 oz (30 ml)
champagne	20	80	1	4	4 oz (114 ml)
chartreuse	120	120	4	4	1 oz (30 ml)
cherry brandy	70	70	3	3	1 oz (30 ml)
cider					
dry	10	100	½	5	½ pt (284 ml)
sweet	10	100	½	5	½ pt (284 ml)
vintage	30	300	1½	10	½ pt (284 ml)
cognac	65	65	3	3	1 oz (30 ml)
cointreau	95	95	4	4	1 oz (30 ml)
crème de cacao	90	90	3	3	1 oz (30 ml)
crème de menthe	90	90	3	3	1 oz (30 ml)
curaçao	90	90	3	3	1 oz (30 ml)
gin	65	65	3	3	1 oz (30 ml)
grand marnier	90	90	3	3	1 oz (30 ml)
Irish coffee	40	200	1	5	¼ pt (142 ml)

Alcoholic drinks/keg bitter

	Calories per 1 oz (30 g)	Calories per portion	Carbohydrate units per 1 oz (30 g)	Carbohydrate units per portion	Size of average portion
keg bitter	10	100	½	5	½ pt (284 ml)
kirsch	65	65	3	3	1 oz (30 ml)
lager, bottled	10	100	½	3	½ pt (284 ml)
madeira	35	35	1½	1½	1 oz (30 ml)
ouzo	65	65	3	3	1 oz (30 ml)
pastis	70	70	3	3	1 oz (30 ml)
port	45	90	2	4	2 oz (57 ml)
retsina	20	100	1	5	¼ pt (142 ml)
rum					
white	65	65	3	3	1 oz (30 ml)
dark	65	65	3	3	1 oz (30 ml)
sangria	20	100	1	5	¼ pt (142 ml)
schnapps	65	65	3	3	1 oz (30 ml)
screw driver	45	220	2	10	¼ pt (142 ml)
shandy	10	80	¾	4	½ pt (284 ml)
sherry					
dry	35	70	1½	3	2 oz (57 ml)
medium	35	70	1¾	3½	2 oz (57 ml)
sweet	40	80	2	4	2 oz (57 ml)
stout	10	100	½	5½	½ pt (284 ml)
Tia Maria	90	90	3	3	1 oz (30 ml)
Tom Collins	25	250	¾	8	½ pt (284 ml)
vermouth					
dry	35	70	2	4	2 oz (57 ml)
sweet	45	90	2½	5	2 oz (57 ml)
vodka	65	65	3	3	1 oz (30 ml)

	Calories per 1 oz (30 g)	Calories per portion	Carbohydrate units per 1 oz (30 g)	Carbohydrate units per portion	Size of average portion
vodka cocktail	50	160	2	6	3 oz (85 ml)
whisky	65	65	3	3	1 oz (30 ml)
whisky sour	55	240	2½	11	4½ oz (128 ml)
wine					
red	20	100	1	5	¼ pt (142 ml)
rosé	20	100	1	5	¼ pt (142 ml)
white, dry	20	100	1	5	¼ pt (142 ml)
white, medium	20	100	1	5	¼ pt (142 ml)
white, sweet	25	125	1½	7	¼ pt (142 ml)
white, sparkling	20	100	1	5	¼ pt (142 ml)
ale					
brown, bottled	10	100	½	3	½ pt (284 ml)
pale, bottled	10	100	½	5	½ pt (284 ml)
strong	20	200	1	10	½ pt (284 ml)
almonds	160	320	¼	½	2 oz (57 g)
almond paste	125	125	3	3	1 oz (30 g)
anchovy					
raw	55	55	0	0	1 oz (30 g)
canned in oil or brine	55	55	0	0	1 oz (30 g)
apples					
raw	10	60	½	q½	1 medium
chutney	55	55	3	3	1 oz (30 g)
cooking, raw	10	60	½	1½	1 medium
stewed, no sugar	10	50	½	2½	5 oz (142 g)
stewed + sugar	20	100	1	5	5 oz (142 g)
baked + sugar	10	60	½	3½	6 oz (171 g)

	Calories per 1 oz (30 g)	Calories per portion	Carbohydrate units per 1 oz (30 g)	Carbohydrate units per portion	Size of average portion
sauce	15	30	3	6	2 oz (57 g)
apple crumble	60	480	2	16	8 oz (227 g)
apples dried	65	65	3½	3½	1 oz (30 g)
apple juice, natural	15	65	¾	3½	¼ pt (142 ml)
apple pie	50	300	1½	7½	6 oz (171 g)
apricots					
raw	5	10	½	½	1 medium
stewed, no sugar	5	35	¼	1½	5 oz (142 g)
stewed + sugar	15	85	1	4½	5 oz (142 g)
canned	30	120	1½	6	4 oz (114 g)
apricots, dried					
raw	50	50	2½	2½	1 oz (30 g)
stewed, no sugar	20	100	1	6	5 oz (142 g)
stewed + sugar	25	125	1	7	5 oz (142 g)
apricot jam	75	20	4	1	1 tsp
armagnac	65	65	3	3	1 oz (30 ml)
arrow root	100	100	5½	5½	1 oz (30 g)
artichokes					
globe, boiled	5	10	¼	½	1 medium
heart, boiled	4	15	0	½	4 oz (114 g)
canned	4	15	0	½	4 oz (114 g)
Jerusalem, boiled	5	20	¼	1	4 oz (114 g)
asparagus					
boiled	5	20	0	¼	4 oz (114 g)
canned	3	10	0	¼	4 oz (114 g)

	Calories per 1 oz (30 g)	Calories per portion	Carbohydrate units per 1 oz (30 g)	Carbohydrate units per portion	Size of average portion
aubergine					
fried	35	140	¼	1	4 oz (114 g)
baked	25	100	¼	1	4 oz (114 g)
Austrian smoked cheese	75	75	0	0	1 oz (30 g)
with ham	75	75	0	0	1 oz (30 g)
avocado pear	65	250	0	½	½ large

B

baby French cheese	90	90	0	0	1 oz (30 g)
bacon gammon joint					
raw	65	65	0	0	1 oz (30 g)
boiled	75	300	0	0	4 oz (114 g)
bacon rashers, raw					
back	120	360	0	0	2 rashers
middle	120	360	0	0	2 rashers
streaky	120	240	0	0	2 rashers

Bacon rashers, fried

	Calories per 1 oz (30 g)	Calories per portion	Carbohydrate units per 1 oz (30 g)	Carbohydrate units per portion	Size of average portion
bacon rashers, fried					
back	130	260	0	0	2 rashers
middle	135	270	0	0	2 rashers
streaky	140	210	0	0	2 rashers
bacon rashers, grilled					
back	115	160	0	0	2 rashers
middle	120	190	0	0	2 rashers
streaky	120	130	0	0	2 rashers
baked beans in tomato sauce	20	100	½	3	5 oz (142 g)
bamboo shoots, canned	10	10	¼	¼	1 oz (30 g)
banana, weighed with skin	15	75	¾	3	1 medium
barley, pearl, boiled	35	35	2	2	1 oz (30 g)
barley wine	20	200	1	10	½ pt (284 ml)
bass					
raw	25	25	0	0	1 oz (30 g)
steamed	40	200	0	0	5 oz (142 g)
fried	50	250	0	0	5 oz (142 g)
beans					
French, boiled	2	10	0	0	5 oz (142 g)
runner, boiled	5	20	0	0	4 oz (114 g)
baked, in tomato sauce	20	100	½	3	5 oz (142 g)

28

Beef silverside

	Calories per 1 oz (30 g)	Calories per portion	Carbohydrate units per 1 oz (30 g)	Carbohydrate units per portion	Size of average portion
broad, boiled	15	60	½	2	4 oz (114 g)
butter, boiled	25	100	1	4	4 oz (114 g)
haricot, boiled	25	100	1	4	4 oz (114 g)
mung, raw	65	65	2	2	1 oz (30 g)
cooked, dahl	30	60	¾	1½	2 oz (57 g)
red kidney, boiled	25	100	1	4	4 oz (114 g)
soya, cooked	10	40	¼	1	4 oz (114 g)
beansprouts raw	3	15	0	0	5 oz (142 g)
boiled	3	15	0	0	5 oz (142 g)
canned	5	25	0	0	5 oz (142 g)
béchamel sauce	40	160	½	2	4 oz (114 g)
beef lean, raw	35	35	0	0	1 oz (30 g)
fat, raw	180	180	0	0	1 oz (30 g)
brisket, boiled	95	380	0	0	4 oz (114 g)
corned	60	120	0	0	2 oz (57 g)
forerib, roast	100	400	0	0	4 oz (114 g)
joint, roast	100	400	0	0	4 oz (114 g)
sirloin, roast	80	240	0	0	3 oz (85 g)
beef, minced lean raw	35	35	0	0	1 oz (30 g)
fat raw	65	65	0	0	1 oz (30 g)
stewed	65	260	0	0	4 oz (114 g)
beef silverside boiled	70	280	0	0	4 oz (114 g)

29

	Calories per 1 oz (30 g)	Calories per portion	Carbohydrate units per 1 oz (30 g)	Carbohydrate units per portion	Size of average portion
boiled, lean only	50	200	0	0	4 oz (114 g)
beef steak					
raw	55	55	0	0	1 oz (30 g)
grilled	55	330	0	0	6 oz (171 g) weighed raw
fried	65	390	0	0	6 oz (171 g) weighed raw
beef stewing steak					
raw	50	50	0	0	1 oz (30 g)
stewed	65	260	0	0	4 oz (114 g)
beefburgers					
fried	75	300	0	0	1 average
grilled	75	290	0	1	1 average
beef extract, concentrated	50	10	0	0	1 tsp
beef sausages					
fried	75	150	½	1	1 sausage
grilled	55	110	½	1	1 sausage
beef steak pudding	65	390	1	6	6 oz (171 g)
beef stew	35	340	¼	2	10 oz (284 g)
beer					
canned bitter	10	100	½	5	½ pt (284 ml)
draught bitter	10	100	½	5	½ pt (284 ml)
draught mild	5	50	¼	3	½ pt (284 ml)
beetroot	15	30	½	1	2 oz (57 g)
bel paese	80	80	0	0	1 oz (30 g)

	Calories per 1 oz (30 g)	Calories per portion	Carbohydrate units per 1 oz (30 g)	Carbohydrate units per portion	Size of average portion
benedictine	110	110	5	5	1 oz (30 ml)
Bengal gram					
raw	90	90	3	3	1 oz (30 g)
cooked (dahl)	40	80	1	2	2 oz (57 g)
bilberries, raw	15	65	¾	3	4 oz (114 g)

BISCUITS AND BUNS

bourbon	120	60	3	1½	1 biscuit
butter biscuit	140	70	3	1½	1 biscuit
Chelsea bun	95	380	3	11½	1 bun
chocolate covered	150	120	4	3½	1 biscuit
coconut	100	50	3	1½	1 biscuit
cream crackers	125	40	4	1½	1 cracker
crispbread					
rye	90	25	4	1	1 biscuit
wheat starch reduced	110	30	2	½	1 biscuit
currant bun					
plain	85	340	3	12½	1 bun
iced	90	360	3½	13½	1 bun
custard cream	120	60	3	1½	1 biscuit
digestive					
plain	135	70	3½	2	1 biscuit
chocolate	140	130	3½	3½	1 biscuit
doughnut					
plain	105	420	2½	9	1 doughnut

	Calories per 1 oz (30 g)	Calories per portion	Carbohydrate units per 1 oz (30 g)	Carbohydrate units per portion	Size of average portion
with jam	115	450	3	11	1 doughnut
fruit shortcake	150	50	4½	1½	1 biscuit
gingernuts	130	65	4½	2	1 biscuit
grissini	85	15	3½	1	1 stick
hot cross bun	80	310	2½	10	1 bun
ice cream cone	75	25	15	5	1 cone
ice cream wafer	75	10	15	3	1 wafer
macaroon	100	200	2½	5	1 large
matzo	110	110	5	5	1 oz (30 g)
oatcakes	125	60	3½	2	1 biscuit
palmier	160	55	3	1	1 biscuit
rock bun	105	420	3½	14	1 bun
sandwich biscuit	145	95	4	2½	1 biscuit
semi sweet, e.g. rich tea	130	50	4½	1½	1 biscuit
shortbread	145	95	3½	2½	1 biscuit
sponge biscuit chocolate covered	150	50	6	2	1 biscuit
sweet	135	55	3½	1½	1 biscuit
wafers filled	150	70	4	1½	1 wafer
water biscuit	125	60	4½	2	1 biscuit
bitter lemon	10	40	½	2	4 oz (114 ml)
blackberries raw	10	35	¼	1	4 oz (114 g)
stewed, no sugar	5	30	¼	1	4 oz (114 g)

	Calories per 1 oz (30 g)	Calories per portion	Carbohydrate units per 1 oz (30 g)	Carbohydrate units per portion	Size of average portion
stewed + sugar	15	65	¾	3½	4 oz (114 g)
canned in syrup	15	65	¾	3½	4 oz (114 g)
jam	75	20	4	1	1 tsp
black pudding, fried	90	350	¾	3½	4 oz (114 g)
blackcurrants					
raw	10	35	¼	1	4 oz (114 g)
stewed, no sugar	5	25	¼	1	4 oz (114 g)
stewed + sugar	15	65	¾	3½	4 oz (114 g)
canned in syrup	20	80	1	5	4 oz (114 g)
jam or jelly	75	20	4	1	1 tsp
juice, undiluted	65	65	3½	3½	1 oz (30 g)
blackcurrant liqueur	70	70	3	3	1 oz (3 ml)
blancmange	35	200	1	6½	6 oz (171 g)
bloater, grilled	70	420	0	0	6 oz (171 g)
Bloody Mary	30	210	1¼	9	7 oz (199 ml)
boiled sweets	95	95	5	5	1 oz (30 g)
bolognese sauce	40	240	¼	1	6 oz (171 g)
Bombay duck					
dried	70	25	0	0	1 fish
fried	120	40	0	0	1 fish
bourbon	65	65	3	3	1 oz (30 ml)
bourbon biscuit	120	60	3	1½	1 biscuit
brain					
calf, boiled	45	135	0	0	3 oz (85 g)
lamb, boiled	35	105	0	0	3 oz (85 g)

	Calories per 1 oz (30 g)	Calories per portion	Carbohydrate units per 1 oz (30 g)	Carbohydrate units per portion	Size of average portion
bran, millers'	55	20	1½	½	1 dsp
bran cereal	80	160	2½	5	2 oz (57 g)
bran flakes	100	100	4½	4½	1 oz (30 g)
bran wheat	60	20	1½	½	1 tbsp
brawn	45	90	0	0	2 oz (57 g)
Brazil nuts	175	350	¼	½	2 oz (57 g)
bread					
bap	90	270	5	9½	1 medium
brown	65	65	2½	2½	1 oz (30 g)
croissant	105	260	2½	6	1 croissant
crumpet	75	110	2	3	1 crumpet
currant	70	70	3	3	1 oz (30 g)
granary	60	60	2	2	1 oz (30 g)
hovis	65	65	2½	2½	1 oz (30 g)
malt	70	70	3	3	1 oz (30 g)
muffins	65	130	3	5½	1 muffin
bread roll					
brown, crusty	80	160	3½	6	1 small
brown, soft	80	160	2½	5	1 small
white, crusty	80	160	3½	7	1 small
white, soft	85	170	3	6	1 small
starch-reduced	110	25	2½	½	1 roll
rye, light	70	70	3	3	1 oz (30 g)
rye, dark	90	90	3½	3½	1 oz (30 g)
soda	60	60	1	1	1 oz (30 g)
white	70	70	3	3	1 oz (30 g)

	Calories per 1 oz (30 g)	Calories per portion	Carbohydrate units per 1 oz (30 g)	Carbohydrate units per portion	Size of average portion
white, fried	180	180	3	3	1 oz (30 g)
white, toasted	85	85	3½	3½	1 oz (30 g)
white, crumbs, dried	100	100	4½	4½	1 oz (30 g)
wholemeal	60	60	2½	2½	1 oz (30 g)
bread sauce	30	60	¾	1½	2 oz (57 g)

BREAKFAST CEREALS

bran cereals	80	160	2½	5	2 oz (57 g)
bran flakes	100	100	4½	4½	1 oz (30 g)
corn flakes	105	105	5	5	1 oz (30 g)
corn flakes, high-protein	110	55	4½	2	½ oz (14 g)
crisped rice	105	50	5	2½	½ oz (14 g)
flaked wheat biscuits	95	50	4	2	1 biscuit
grapenuts	100	100	4½	4½	1 oz (30 g)
instant porridge	110	110	4	4	1 oz (30 g)
muesli	105	210	4	8	2 oz (57 g)
puffed wheat	95	95	4	4	1 oz (30 g)
raisin bran	100	100	4½	4½	1 oz (30 g)
shredded wheat	90	90	4	4	1 oz (30 g)
sugar-coated puffed wheat	100	100	5	5	1 oz (30 g)
bream raw	25	25	0	0	1 oz (30 g)

Bream

	Calories per 1 oz (30 g)	Calories per portion	Carbohydrate units per 1 oz (30 g)	Carbohydrate units per portion	Size of average portion
steamed	40	190	0	0	5 oz (142 g)
fried	50	240	0	0	5 oz (142 g)
brie	85	85	0	0	1 oz (30 g)
brioche	90	220	2	5	1 roll
broad beans, boiled	15	60	½	2	4 oz (114 g)
broccoli tops, boiled	5	20	0	0	4 oz (114 g)
brown ale, bottled	10	100	½	3	½ pt (284 ml)
brown sauce, bottled	30	5	1½	½	1 tsp
Brussels sprouts, boiled	5	30	0	0	6 oz (171 g)
bun, currant plain	85	340	3	12½	1 bun
iced	90	360	3½	13½	1 bun
butter, salted & unsalted	210	50	0	0	1 pat
butter beans, boiled	25	100	1	4	4 oz (114 g)
butter biscuits	140	70	3	1½	1 biscuit
buttermilk	10	50	0	1	¼ pt (142 ml)

36

	Calories per 1 oz (30 g)	Calories per portion	Carbohydrate units per 1 oz (30 g)	Carbohydrate units per portion	Size of average portion

C

cabbage					
red raw	5	20	0	0	3 oz (85 g)
boiled	4	15	0	0	4 oz (114 g)
pickled	5	5	0	0	1 oz (30 g)
savoy, boiled	3	10	0	0	4 oz (114 g)
white, raw	3	10	0	0	4 oz (114 g)
white, boiled	4	15	0	0	4 oz (114 g)
caerphilly	100	100	0	0	1 oz (30 g)

CAKES AND PASTRIES

angel cake	60	240	2½	11	4 oz (114 g)
apple pie	50	300	1½	7½	6 oz (171 g)
apple strudel	60	230	1½	6½	4 oz (114 g)
bakewell tart	120	480	2½	10	4 oz (114 g)
battenburg cake	115	450	2½	10	4 oz (114 g) ·
cheese cake					
lemon	120	430	1	4½	4 oz (114 g)

37

	Calories per 1 oz (30 g)	Calories per portion	Carbohydrate units per 1 oz (30 g)	Carbohydrate units per portion	Size of average portion
currant	105	420	1½	5	4 oz (114 g)
cherry cake	90	350	2	7	4 oz (114 g)
chocolate cake iced, filled	85	330	2½	10	4 oz (114 g)
chocolate cup cake	115	230	3	6	1 cake
Christmas cake	90	360	3	12	4 oz (114 g)
custard tart	95	370	2	7	4 oz (114 g)
Danish pastry, apricot filling	105	210	2½	5	1 small
date & walnut loaf	80	310	3	11½	4 oz (114 g)
dumpling-suet	60	180	1½	4½	1 medium
Dundee cake	100	390	2½	11	4 oz (114 g)
eccles	75	150	2	4	1 small
éclair	105	210	2	4	1 small
fairy	105	105	3½	3½	1 small
fancy iced cake	115	230	4	8	1 cake
fruit cake rich	95	280	3	9	3 oz (85 g)
iced	100	300	3½	10	3 oz (85 g)
plain	100	300	3	9	3 oz (85 g)
gingerbread	105	315	3½	10	3 oz (85 g)
jam tart	120	120	3½	3½	1 tart
lardy cake	105	410	3½	14½	4 oz (114 g)
madeira cake	110	330	3½	10	3 oz (85 g)
meringue	110	50	5½	2½	1 large
mince pie	125	210	3½	6	1 pie

	Calories per 1 oz (30 g)	Calories per portion	Carbohydrate units per 1 oz (30 g)	Carbohydrate units per portion	Size of average portion
pastry, choux					
raw	60	60	1	1	1 oz (30 g)
cooked	95	95	1½	1½	1 oz (30 g)
pastry, flaky					
raw	120	120	2	2	1 oz (30 g)
cooked	160	160	2½	2½	1 oz (30 g)
pastry, short					
raw	130	130	2½	2½	1 oz (30 g)
cooked	150	150	3	3	1 oz (30 g)
scones					
plain	85	130	2½	4	1 medium
cheese	100	200	2½	4½	1 medium
currant	105	160	3½	5	1 medium
scotch pancakes, without butter	80	120	2	3	1 medium
sponge cake					
with fat	130	260	3	6	2 oz (57 g)
fatless	85	170	3	6	2 oz (57 g)
with jam	85	170	3½	7	2 oz (57 g)
simnel cake	110	440	3	12	4 oz (114 g)
Swiss roll	75	290	3	12	4 oz (114 g)
tea cake	85	170	3	6	1 tea cake
treacle tart	105	420	3½	14	4 oz (114 g)
calvados	70	70	3	3	1 oz (30 ml)
camembert	85	85	0	0	1 oz (30 g)

	Calories per 1 oz (30 g)	Calories per portion	Carbohydrate units per 1 oz (30 g)	Carbohydrate units per portion	Size of average portion
capers	0	0	0	0	1 oz (30 g)
carp					
raw	25	25	0	0	1 oz (30 g)
steamed	40	190	0	0	5 oz (142 g)
fried	50	240	0	0	5 oz (142 g)
carrots					
old, raw	5	20	¼	1	4 oz (114 g)
old, boiled	5	20	¼	1	4 oz (114 g)
young, raw	5	30	½	1	4 oz (114 g)
young, boiled	4	15	¼	1	4 oz (114 g)
young, canned	5	20	¼	1	4 oz (114 g)
carrot juice	5	25	½	2	¼ pt (142 ml)
cashew nuts	155	610	1	3½	4 oz (142 ml)
cassata	45	95	1½	3	2 oz (57 g)
cassis	70	70	3	3	1 oz (30 ml)
cauliflower					
raw	4	15	0	0	4 oz (114 g)
boiled	3	10	0	0	4 oz (114 g)
pickled	3	3	0	0	1 oz (30 g)
cauliflower cheese	30	255	¼	2	8 oz (227 g)
caviar					
red	60	60	0	0	1 oz (30 g)
black	60	60	0	0	1 oz (30 g)
grey	60	60	0	0	1 oz (30 g)
celeriac					
raw	5	10	0	0	2 oz (57 g)

	Calories per 1 oz (30 g)	Calories per portion	Carbohydrate units per 1 oz (30 g)	Carbohydrate units per portion	Size of average portion
boiled	4	15	0	0	4 oz (114 g)
Celery					
raw	2	5	0	0	2 oz (57 g)
boiled	2	5	0	0	2 oz (57 g)
canned	1	5	0	0	4 oz (114 g)
champagne	20	80	1	4	4 oz (114 ml)
chapatis					
with fat	95	475	3	15	1 large
fatless	60	285	2½	12½	1 large
chartreuse	120	120	4	4	1 oz (30 ml)
CHEESE					
Austrian-smoked	75	75	0	0	1 oz (30 g)
with ham	75	75	0	0	1 oz (30 g)
baby French, soft	90	90	0	0	1 oz (30 g)
bel paese	80	80	0	0	1 oz (30 g)
boursin					
with herbs	110	110	0	0	1 oz (30 g)
with pepper	110	110	0	0	1 oz (30 g)
caerphilly	100	100	0	0	1 oz (30 g)
camembert	85	85	0	0	1 oz (30 g)
cheddar	120	120	0	0	1 oz (30 g)
cheshire	120	120	0	0	1 oz (30 g)
cottage cheese					
plain	25	100	0	0	small carton
+ chives	25	100	0	0	small carton

	Calories per 1 oz (30 g)	Calories per portion	Carbohydrate units per 1 oz (30 g)	Carbohydrate units per portion	Size of average portion
+ onions & peppers	25	100	0	0	small carton
+ pineapple	25	100	0	1	small carton
cream	125	125	0	0	1 oz (30 g)
danbo	95	95	0	0	1 oz (30 g)
Danish blue	100	100	0	0	1 oz (30 g)
dolcelatte	95	95	0	0	1 oz (30 g)
double gloucester	100	100	0	0	1 oz (30 g)
edam	85	85	0	0	1 oz (30 g)
emmenthal	110	110	0	0	1 oz (30 g)
esrom	90	90	0	0	1 oz (30 g)
gorgonzola	100	100	0	0	1 oz (30 g)
gouda	85	85	0	0	1 oz (30 g)
gruyère	130	130	0	0	1 oz (30 g)
lancashire	100	100	0	0	1 oz (30 g)
leicester	110	110	0	0	1 oz (30 g)
mozzarella	95	95	0	0	1 oz (30 g)
parmesan	120	20	0	0	2 tsp
Port Salut	90	90	0	0	1 oz (30 g)
processed	90	90	0	0	1 oz (30 g)
ricotta	70	70	0	0	1 oz (30 g)
roquefort	100	100	0	0	1 oz (30 g)
sage derby	110	110	0	0	1 oz (30 g)
St. Paulin	90	90	0	0	1 oz (30 g)
stilton blue	130	130	0	0	1 oz (30 g)
tomé au raisin	80	80	0	0	1 oz (30 g)
wensleydale	110	110	0	0	1 oz (30 g)

	Calories per 1 oz (30 g)	Calories per portion	Carbohydrate units per 1 oz (30 g)	Carbohydrate units per portion	Size of average portion
cheese cake					
lemon	120	430	1	4½	4 oz (114 g)
currant	105	420	1½	5	4 oz (114 g)
cheese football	150	15	5	½	1 football
cheese pudding	50	300	½	3	6 oz (171 g)
cheese sauce	55	280	½	2½	5 oz (142 g)
cheese soufflé	70	355	½	3	5 oz (142 g)
cheese spread	80	80	0	0	1 portion
cheese straws	160	160	1½	1½	1 oz (30 g)
chelsea bun	95	380	3	11½	1 bun
cherries					
eating, raw	10	45	½	2	4 oz (114 g)
cooking, raw	10	45	½	2	4 oz (114 g)
stewed, no sugar	10	45	½	2	4 oz (114 g)
stewed + sugar	20	80	1	4	4 oz (114 g)
canned	20	80	1	4	4 oz (114 g)
glacé	60	10	3	½	1 cherry
cherry jam	75	20	4	1	1 tsp
cherry brandy	70	70	3	3	1 oz (30 ml)
cheshire cheese	120	120	0	0	1 oz (30 g)
chestnuts	50	100	2	4	2 oz (57 g)
chickpeas					
raw	90	90	3	3	1 oz (30 g)
cooked, dahl	40	160	1	4	4 oz (114 g)
chicken					
raw, meat only	35	35	0	0	1 oz (30 g)

Chicken

	Calories per 1 oz (30 g)	Calories per portion	Carbohydrate units per 1 oz (30 g)	Carbohydrate units per portion	Size of average portion
raw, meat & skin	65	65	0	0	1 oz (30 g)
chicken: boiled					
meat only	50	255	0	0	5 oz (142 g)
light meat	45	230	0	0	5 oz (142 g)
dark meat	60	295	0	0	5 oz (142 g)
chicken: roast					
meat only	40	210	0	0	5 oz (142 g)
meat & skin	60	290	0	0	5 oz (142 g)
light meat	40	200	0	0	5 oz (142 g)
dark meat	45	220	0	0	5 oz (142 g)
wing quarter	20	65	0	0	1 medium
leg quarter	25	155	0	0	1 small
chicken cream soup	15	140	0	2	½ pt (284 ml)
chicken noodle soup	5	55	0	2	½ pt (284 ml)
chicory					
raw	3	5	0	0	2 oz (57 g)
boiled	3	10	0	0	4 oz (114 g)
chips, potato					
fresh	70	430	2	12	6 oz (171 g)
frozen	80	495	2	10	6 oz (171 g)
chocolate					
milk	150	250	3½	6	small bar
plain	150	250	3½	6	small bar
fancy	130	520	4	15	4 oz (114 g)
drinking	105	35	4	1½	2 tsp
biscuit, full coated	150	120	4	3½	1 biscuit

	Calories per 1 oz (30 g)	Calories per portion	Carbohydrate units per 1 oz (30 g)	Carbohydrate units per portion	Size of average portion
chocolate ice cream	45	95	1½	3	2 oz (57 g)
chocolate malted milk powder	105	35	4½	1½	1 tsp
chocolate mousse, frozen	35	100	1	3	3½ oz (100 g)
choux pastry, raw	60	60	1	1	1 oz (30 g)
cooked	95	95	1½	1½	1 oz (30 g)
Christmas cake	90	360	3	12	4 oz (114 g)
Christmas pudding	85	340	2½	10	4 oz (114 g)
chutney apple	55	55	3	3	1 oz (30 g)
mango	55	55	3	3	1 oz (30 g)
tomato	45	45	2	2	1 oz (30 g)
cider dry	10	100	½	5	½ pt (284 ml)
sweet	10	100	½	5	½ pt (284 ml)
vintage	30	300	1½	10	½ pt (284 ml)
clam raw	20	20	0	0	1 oz (30 g)
steamed	30	60	0	0	2 oz (57 g)
canned	30	60	0	0	2 oz (57 g)
clementine	10	10	½	½	1 small
clotted cream	160	160	0	0	1 oz (30 g)
cockles shelled, raw	10	10	0	0	1 oz (30 g)

Cockles

	Calories per 1 oz (30 g)	Calories per portion	Carbohydrate units per 1 oz (30 g)	Carbohydrate units per portion	Size of average portion
boiled	15	30	0	0	2 oz (57 g)
canned	15	30	0	0	2 oz (57 g)
cocoa powder	90	15	¾	0	1 tsp
coconut					
dessicated	175	175	1½	1½	1 oz (30 g)
fresh	100	100	¼	¼	1 oz (30 g)
milk	5	10	¼	½	2 oz (57 g)
oil	255	255	0	0	1 oz (30 g)
coconut biscuit	100	50	3	1½	1 biscuit
cod					
raw	20	20	0	0	1 oz (30 g)
steamed	25	130	0	0	5 oz (142 g)
fried	35	180	0	0	5 oz (142 g)
fried in batter	55	340	½	2	6 oz (171 g)
fried in breadcrumbs	50	300	0	0	6 oz (171 g)
cod roe					
fried	55	110	¾	1½	2 oz (57 g)
smoked	30	30	0	0	1 oz (30 g)
cod liver oil	255	40	0	0	1 tsp
coffee & chicory essence	60	10	3	½	1 tsp
coffee, ground, with water	0	2	0	0	1 cup
coffee instant	30	1	0	0	1 tsp
coffee Irish	40	200	1	5	¼ pt (142 ml)
cognac	65	65	3	3	1 oz (30 ml)

	Calories per 1 oz (30 g)	Calories per portion	Carbohydrate units per 1 oz (30 g)	Carbohydrate units per portion	Size of average portion
cointreau	85	95	4	4	1 oz (30 ml)
cola drink	10	110	½	5	½ pt (284 ml)
coleslaw	20	70	0	1	4 oz (114 g)
condensed milk whole, sweetened	90	90	3	3	1 oz (30 ml)
skimmed, sweetened	75	75	3½	3½	1 oz (30 ml)
consommé	10	70	0	0	½ pt (284 ml)
corn oil	255	255	0	0	1 oz (30 ml)
corn on the cob, boiled	35	175	1	6	1 medium
corned beef	60	120	0	0	2 oz (57 g)
corn flakes	105	105	5	5	1 oz (30 g)
cornflour	100	15	5	1	1 tsp
cornish pasty	95	570	2	11	6 oz (171 g)
cottage cheese plain	25	100	0	0	small carton
+ chives	25	100	0	0	small carton
+ onions & pepper	25	100	0	0	small carton
+ pineapple	25	100	0	1	small carton
courgette raw	3	3	0	0	1 oz (30 g)
boiled	1	5	0	0	4 oz (114 g)
fried	35	140	0	½	4 oz (114 g)
crab boiled	35	140	0	0	4 oz (114 g)
canned	25	100	0	0	4 oz (114 g)

	Calories per 1 oz (30 g)	Calories per portion	Carbohydrate units per 1 oz (30 g)	Carbohydrate units per portion	Size of average portion
cranberries					
raw	4	4	¼	¼	1 oz (30 g)
sauce or jelly	40	20	2	1	1 dsp
crayfish					
in shells	10	70	0	0	6 oz (171 g)
shelled	30	60	0	0	2 oz (57 g)
cream					
clotted	160	160	0	0	1 oz (30 ml)
double	125	510	0	0	small carton
single	60	240	¼	1	small carton
soured	55	55	0	0	1 oz (30 ml)
sterilized	65	65	¼	¼	1 oz (30 ml)
whipping	95	95	0	0	1 oz (30 ml)
cream cheese	125	125	0	0	1 oz (30 ml)
cream crackers	125	40	4	1½	1 cracker
crème de menthe	90	90	3	3	1 oz (30 ml)
crispbread					
rye	90	25	4	1	1 biscuit
starch reduced	110	30	2	½	1 biscuit
crisped rice breakfast cereal	105	50	5	2½	½ oz (14 g)
crisps, potato	150	125	3	2½	small pkt
croissant	105	260	2½	6	1 croissant
crumpet	75	110	2	3	1 crumpet
cucumber					
raw	3	3	0	0	1 oz (30 g)

	Calories per 1 oz (30 g)	Calories per portion	Carbohydrate units per 1 oz (30 g)	Carbohydrate units per portion	Size of average portion
pickled	3	3	¼	¼	1 oz (30 g)
curaçao	90	90	3	3	1 oz (30 ml)
curd cheese	25	25	0	0	1 oz (30 g)
currant bun plain	85	340	3	12½	1 bun
iced	90	360	3½	13½	1 bun
curried meat	45	270	½	2½	6 oz (171 g)
curry powder	65	65	1½	1½	1 oz (30 g)
custard, egg	35	135	½	2½	4 oz (114 g)
custard cream biscuit	120	60	3	1½	1 biscuit
custard powder	100	100	5	5	1 oz (30 g)
boiled	35	170	1	5	5 oz (142 g)
custard tart	95	370	2	7	4 oz (114 g)

dahl (cooked chickpeas)	40	160	1	4	4 oz (114 g)

	Calories per 1 oz (30 g)	Calories per portion	Carbohydrate units per 1 oz (30 g)	Carbohydrate units per portion	Size of average portion
dahl (cooked mung beans)	30	60	¾	1½	2 oz (57 g)
dahl, masur (cooked lentils)	25	105	¾	2½	4 oz (114 g)
damsons					
raw	10	40	½	2	4 oz (114 g)
stewed, no sugar	10	40	½	2	4 oz (114 g)
stewed + sugar	20	80	1	4	4 oz (114 g)
danbo cheese	95	95	0	0	1 oz (30 g)
Danish blue cheese	100	100	0	0	1 oz (30 g)
Danish pastry, apricot filling	105	210	2½	5	1 small
dates, dried	60	120	3	6	2 oz (57 g)
date & walnut loaf	80	310	3	11½	4 oz (114 g)
desiccated coconut	175	175	1½	1½	1 oz (30 g)
digestive biscuit					
chocolate	140	130	3½	3½	1 biscuit
plain	135	70	3½	2	1 biscuit
dogfish, fried in batter	75	375	½	2	5 oz (142 g)
dolcelatte cheese	95	95	0	0	1 oz (30 g)
double gloucester cheese	100	100	0	0	1 oz (30 g)
doughnuts					
plain	105	420	2½	9	1 doughnut
with jam	115	450	3	11	1 doughnut

	Calories per 1 oz (30 g)	Calories per portion	Carbohydrate units per 1 oz (30 g)	Carbohydrate units per portion	Size of average portion
drambuie	65	65	3	3	1 oz (30 ml)
dried milk					
whole	140	35	2	½	2 tsp
skimmed	100	15	3	½	2 tsp
drinking chocolate	105	35	4	1½	2 tsp
dripping, beef	255	255	0	0	1 oz (30 g)
drop scones	80	120	2	3	1 small
duck					
raw meat only	35	35	0	0	1 oz (30 g)
roast meat only	55	270	0	0	5 oz (142 g)
dumpling-suet	60	180	1½	4½	1 medium
Dundee cake	100	390	2½	11	4 oz (114 g)

eccles cake	75	150	2	4	1 small
éclair	105	210	2	4	1 small
edam cheese	85	85	0	0	1 oz (30 g)

	Calories per 1 oz (30 g)	Calories per portion	Carbohydrate units per 1 oz (30 g)	Carbohydrate units per portion	Size of average portion
eel					
raw	50	50	0	0	1 oz (30 g)
fried	70	340	0	0	5 oz (142 g)
fried in batter	70	350	¼	1½	6 oz (171 g)
jellied	60	230	0	0	4 oz (114 g)
smoked	55	110	0	0	2 oz (57 g)
steamed	55	280	0	0	5 oz (142 g)
egg custard	35	135	½	2½	4 oz (114 g)
eggplant					
fried	35	140	¼	1	4 oz (114 g)
baked	25	100	¼	1	4 oz (114 g)
egg					
whole, raw	40	80	0	0	1 large
white, raw	10	15	0	0	1 large
yolk, raw	95	80	0	0	1 large
whole, boiled	40	80	0	0	1 large
whole, fried	65	130	0	0	1 large
whole, poached	45	90	0	0	1 large
scrambled	70	140	0	0	1 large
emmenthal cheese	110	110	0	0	1 oz (30 g)
endive					
raw	3	5	0	0	2 oz (57 g)
boiled	3	10	0	0	4 oz (114 g)
evaporated milk, whole, unsweetened	45	45	¾	¾	1 oz (30 ml)

F

	Calories per 1 oz (30 g)	Calories per portion	Carbohydrate units per 1 oz (30 g)	Carbohydrate units per portion	Size of average portion
faggots	75	600	¾	7	2 faggots
fairy cake	105	105	3½	3½	1 small
fancy iced cakes	115	230	4	8	1 small
figs					
green, raw	10	15	¾	1	1 fig
dried, raw	60	45	3	2½	1 fig
stewed, no sugar	35	170	1½	8	5 oz (142 g)
stewed + sugar	40	195	2	10	5 oz (142 g)
FISH					
abalone					
raw	30	30	0	0	1 oz (30 g)
steamed/canned	25	125	0	0	5 oz (142 g)
fried	35	175	0	0	5 oz (142 g)
anchovy					
raw	55	55	0	0	1 oz (30 g)

	Calories per 1 oz (30 g)	Calories per portion	Carbohydrate units per 1 oz (30 g)	Carbohydrate units per portion	Size of average portion
canned in oil or brine	55	55	0	0	1 oz (30 g)
bass					
raw	25	25	0	0	1 oz (30 g)
steamed	40	200	0	0	5 oz (142 g)
fried	50	250	0	0	5 oz (142 g)
bloater, grilled	70	420	0	0	6 oz (171 g)
Bombay duck					
dried	70	25	0	0	1 fish
fried	120	40	0	0	1 fish
bream					
raw	25	25	0	0	1 oz (30 g)
steamed	40	190	0	0	5 oz (142 g)
fried	50	240	0	0	5 oz (142 g)
carp					
raw	25	25	0	0	1 oz (30 g)
steamed	40	190	0	0	5 oz (142 g)
fried	50	240	0	0	5 oz (142 g)
caviar					
red, black, grey	60	60	0	0	1 oz (30 g)
clam					
raw	20	20	0	0	1 oz (30 g)
steamed	30	60	0	0	5 oz (142 g)
canned	30	60	0	0	5 oz (142 g)
cockles					
shelled, raw	10	10	0	0	1 oz (30 g)
boiled	15	30	0	0	2 oz (57 g)

	Calories per 1 oz (30 g)	Calories per portion	Carbohydrate units per 1 oz (30 g)	Carbohydrate units per portion	Size of average portion
cod					
raw	20	20	0	0	1 oz (30 g)
steamed	25	130	0	0	5 oz (142 g)
fried	35	180	0	0	5 oz (142 g)
fried in batter	55	340	½	2	6 oz (171 g)
in breadcrumbs	50	300	0	0	6 oz (171 g)
cod roe					
fried	55	110	¾	1½	2 oz (57 g)
smoked	30	30	0	0	1 oz (30 g)
crab					
boiled	35	140	0	0	4 oz (114 g)
canned	25	100	0	0	4 oz (114 g)
crayfish					
in shells	10	70	0	0	6 oz (171 g)
shelled	30	60	0	0	6 oz (171 g)
dogfish fried in batter	75	375	½	2	5 oz (142 g)
eel					
raw	50	50	0	0	1 oz (30 g)
fried	70	340	0	0	5 oz (142 g)
fried in batter	70	350	¼	1½	6 oz (171 g)
jellied	60	230	0	0	4 oz (114 g)
smoked	55	110	0	0	2 oz (57 g)
steamed	55	280	0	0	5 oz (142 g)
haddock					
fresh, raw	20	20	0	0	1 oz (30 g)

	Calories per 1 oz (30 g)	Calories per portion	Carbohydrate units per 1 oz (30 g)	Carbohydrate units per portion	Size of average portion
fried	50	250	0	0	5 oz (142 g)
steamed	30	150	0	0	5 oz (142 g)
smoked, raw	20	20	0	0	1 oz (30 g)
steamed	30	145	0	0	5 oz (142 g)
hake raw	20	20	0	0	1 oz (30 g)
poached	30	150	0	0	5 oz (142 g)
halibut raw	25	25	0	0	1 oz (30 g)
steamed	35	185	0	0	5 oz (142 g)
poached	40	190	0	0	5 oz (142 g)
fried	50	240	0	0	5 oz (142 g)
herring raw	65	65	0	0	1 oz (30 g)
steamed	55	280	0	0	5 oz (142 g)
fried in oatmeal	65	330	0	½	5 oz (142 g)
pickled	80	160	0	0	2 oz (57 g)
roe, fried	70	140	¼	½	2 oz (57 g)
kipper raw	80	80	0	0	1 oz (30 g)
baked or steamed	60	290	0	0	5 oz (142 g)
fried	70	340	0	0	5 oz (142 g)
lobster, boiled	35	175	0	0	5 oz (142 g)
mackerel raw	65	65	0	0	1 oz (30 g)
fried	55	275	0	0	5 oz (142 g)

	Calories per 1 oz (30 g)	Calories per portion	Carbohydrate units per 1 oz (30 g)	Carbohydrate units per portion	Size of average portion
steamed	75	380	0	0	5 oz (142 g)
smoked	90	440	0	0	5 oz (142 g)
mullet					
raw	40	40	0	0	1 oz (30 g)
steamed	50	250	0	0	5 oz (142 g)
fried	60	300	0	0	5 oz (142 g)
mussels					
raw	20	20	0	0	1 oz (30 g)
steamed	25	75	0	0	3 oz (85 g)
canned	20	55	0	0	3 oz (85 g)
octopus					
raw	20	20	0	0	1 oz (30 g)
steamed	25	125	0	0	5 oz (142 g)
fried	30	160	0	0	5 oz (142 g)
fried in batter	55	340	½	2½	5 oz (142 g)
oyster					
raw	15	15	0	0	2 oysters
canned	15	45	0	0	6 oysters
smoked	15	45	0	0	3 oz (85 g)
pilchards					
canned in oil	65	250	0	0	4 oz (114 g)
canned in tomato sauce	35	140	0	¼	4 oz (114 g)
plaice					
raw	25	25	0	0	1 oz (30 g)
steamed	25	130	0	0	5 oz (142 g)

	Calories per 1 oz (30 g)	Calories per portion	Carbohydrate units per 1 oz (30 g)	Carbohydrate units per portion	Size of average portion
fried in batter	80	400	¾	4	5 oz (142 g)
fried in breadcrumbs	65	325	½	2½	5 oz (142 g)
prawns					
raw in shells	10	10	0	0	1 oz (30 g)
shelled	30	60	0	0	2 oz (57 g)
boiled	30	60	0	0	2 oz (57 g)
potted	120	240	0	0	2 oz (57 g)
salmon					
raw	50	50	0	0	1 oz (30 g)
steamed	55	280	0	0	5 oz (142 g)
fried	65	330	0	0	5 oz (142 g)
smoked	40	80	0	0	2 oz (57 g)
canned	45	90	0	0	2 oz (57 g)
salmon trout					
raw	50	50	0	0	1 oz (30 g)
poached	55	280	0	0	5 oz (142 g)
sardine					
canned in oil, drained	60	120	0	0	2 oz (57 g)
canned in sauce	50	100	0	0	2 oz (57 g)
scallop					
raw	30	30	0	0	1 oz (30 g)
steamed	30	90	0	0	2 fish
fried	35	115	0	0	2 fish
canned	30	90	0	0	3 oz (85 g)
scampi					
boiled	30	120	0	0	3 pieces

	Calories per 1 oz (30 g)	Calories per portion	Carbohydrate units per 1 oz (30 g)	Carbohydrate units per portion	Size of average portion
fried in batter	55	275	½	2	3 pieces
fried in breadcrumbs	90	450	2	8	3 pieces
skate					
raw	20	20	0	0	1 oz (30 g)
steamed	25	130	0	0	5 oz (142 g)
fried	35	180	0	0	5 oz (142 g)
fried in batter	55	340	½	3	6 oz (171 g)
fried in breadcrumbs	50	350	¼	1	6 oz (171 g)
sole, lemon					
raw	25	25	0	0	1 oz (30 g)
steamed	25	130	0	0	5 oz (142 g)
fried in breadcrumbs	60	310	0	½	5 oz (142 g)
sprats					
raw	25	25	0	0	1 oz (30 g)
fried	125	500	0	0	4 oz (114 g)
fried in batter	125	500	½	2	4 oz (114 g)
squid					
raw	20	20	0	0	1 oz (30 g)
steamed	25	125	0	0	5 oz (142 g)
fried	35	170	0	0	5 oz (142 g)
trout					
raw	25	25	0	0	1 oz (30 g)
steamed	25	200	0	0	1 small
fried	40	320	0	0	1 small
smoked	25	200	0	0	1 small
tuna in oil, drained	80	160	0	0	1 small can

	Calories per 1 oz (30 g)	Calories per portion	Carbohydrate units per 1 oz (30 g)	Carbohydrate units per portion	Size of average portion
turbot					
raw	20	20	0	0	1 oz (30 g)
steamed	30	140	0	0	5 oz (142 g)
fried breadcrumbs	50	250	¼	1	5 oz (142 g)
whitebait					
raw	15	15	0	0	1 oz (30 g)
fried in batter	150	590	½	2	4 oz (114 g)
fried in flour	150	590	¼	1	4 oz (114 g)
whiting					
fried	55	275	½	2	5 oz (142 g)
steamed	25	130	0	0	5 oz (142 g)
winkles					
boiled in shell	4	4	0	0	1 oz (30 g)
shelled	20	60	0	0	3 oz (85 g)
fish cakes					
frozen	30	60	1	2	1 cake
fried	65	130	1	2	1 cake
fish fingers					
frozen	50	100	1	2	2 fingers
fried	65	130	1	2	2 fingers
fish paste	50	10	¼	0	1 tsp
fish pie	35	280	¾	6	8 oz (227 g)
flaked wheat biscuits	95	50	4	2	1 biscuit

	Calories per 1 oz (30 g)	Calories per portion	Carbohydrate units per 1 oz (30 g)	Carbohydrate units per portion	Size of average portion
flaky pastry					
raw	120	120	2½	2½	1 oz (30 g)
cooked	160	160	2½	2½	1 oz (30 g)
flour					
brown	95	95	4	4	1 oz (30 g)
white bread-making	95	95	4	4	1 oz (30 g)
plain	100	100	4½	4½	1 oz (30 g)
self-raising	95	95	4½	4½	1 oz (30 g)
wholemeal	90	90	3½	3½	1 oz (30 g)
frankfurters	80	80	¼	¼	1 small
French beans, boiled	2	10	0	0	5 oz (142 g)
French dressing	185	185	0	0	1 oz (30 ml)
fried bread	180	180	3	3	1 oz (30 g)
frogs' legs					
raw	20	20	0	0	1 oz (30 g)
fried in batter	85	255	0	0	12 legs

FRUIT AND FRUIT JUICES

apples	10	60	½	1½	1 medium
chutney	55	55	3	3	1 oz (30 g)
cooking, raw	10	60	½	1½	1 medium
stewed, no sugar	10	50	½	2½	5 oz (142 g)
stewed + sugar	20	100	1	5	5 oz (142 g)
baked + sugar	10	60	½	3½	6 oz (171 g)

	Calories per 1 oz (30 g)	Calories per portion	Carbohydrate units per 1 oz (30 g)	Carbohydrate units per portion	Size of average portion
dried	65	65	3½	3½	1 oz (30 g)
juice, natural	15	65	¾	3½	¼ pt (142 ml)
sauce, no sugar	15	30	3	6	2 oz (57 g)
apricot fresh, raw	5	10	½	½	1 medium
stewed, no sugar	5	35	¼	1½	5 oz (142 g)
stewed + sugar	15	85	1	4½	5 oz (142 g)
canned	30	120	1½	6	4 oz (114 g)
dried	50	50	2½	2½	1 oz (30 g)
stewed, no sugar	20	100	1	6	5 oz (142 g)
stewed + sugar	25	125	1	7	5 oz (142 g)
avocado pear	65	250	0	½	½ large
banana, weighed with skin	15	75	¾	3	1 medium
bilberries, raw	15	65	¾	3	4 oz (114 g)
blackberries raw	10	35	¼	1	4 oz (114 g)
stewed, no sugar	5	30	¼	1	4 oz (114 g)
stewed + sugar	15	65	¾	3½	4 oz (114 g)
canned in syrup	15	65	¾	3½	4 oz (114 g)
blackcurrants raw	10	35	¼	1	4 oz (114 g)
stewed, no sugar	5	25	¼	1	4 oz (114 g)
stewed + sugar	20	80	1	5	4 oz (114 g)
cherries eating, raw	10	45	½	2	4 oz (114 g)

	Calories per 1 oz (30 g)	Calories per portion	Carbohydrate units per 1 oz (30 g)	Carbohydrate units per portion	Size of average portion
cooking, raw	10	45	½	2	4 oz (114 g)
stewed, no sugar	10	45	½	2	4 oz (114 g)
stewed + sugar	20	80	1	4	4 oz (114 g)
canned	20	80	1	4	4 oz (114 g)
glacé	60	10	3	½	1 cherry
clementine	10	10	½	½	1 small
coconut, shelled, raw	100	100	¼	¼	1 oz (30 g)
cranberries, raw	4	4	¼	¼	1 oz (30 g)
damsons raw	10	40	½	2	4 oz (114 g)
stewed, no sugar	10	40	½	2	4 oz (114 g)
stewed + sugar	20	80	1	4	4 oz (114 g)
dates, dried	60	120	3	6	2 oz (57 g)
figs green, raw	10	15	¾	1	1 fig
dried, raw	60	45	3	2½	1 fig
stewed, no sugar	35	170	1½	8	5 oz (142 g)
stewed + sugar	40	195	2	10	5 oz (142 g)
fruit salad, canned	25	110	1½	6	4 oz (114 g)
gooseberries green, raw	5	20	0	¾	4 oz (114 g)
stewed, no sugar	4	15	0	¾	4 oz (114 g)
stewed + sugar	15	55	¾	3	4 oz (114 g)
ripe, raw	10	40	½	2	4 oz (114 g)
canned	40	120	2	8	4 oz (114 g)

	Calories per 1 oz (30 g)	Calories per portion	Carbohydrate units per 1 oz (30 g)	Carbohydrate units per portion	Size of average portion
grapefruit					
fresh	3	15	¼	2	½ medium
canned	15	65	1	3½	4 oz (114 g)
juice, no sugar	10	50	½	2	¼ pt (142 ml)
juice + sugar	10	55	½	3	¼ pt (142 ml)
grapes					
black or white, raw	20	70	1	4	4 oz (114 g)
juice	20	100	1	9	¼ pt (142 ml)
greengages					
raw	15	15	1	1	1 fruit
stewed, no sugar	10	45	½	2	4 oz (114 g)
stewed + sugar	20	85	1	4	4 oz (114 g)
guava, canned	15	60	1	4	4 oz (114 g)
lemon, whole	5	15	¼	½	1 medium
loganberries					
raw or stewed	5	20	¼	1	4 oz (114 g)
stewed + sugar	15	60	¾	3	4 oz (114 g)
canned	30	110	1½	6	4 oz (114 g)
lychees					
raw	20	20	1	1	1 oz (30 g)
canned	20	80	1	4	4 oz (114 g)
mandarin					
raw	10	25	½	1	1 medium
canned	15	60	1	4	4 oz (114 g)
mango					
raw	15	105	1	6	1 medium

	Calories per 1 oz (30 g)	Calories per portion	Carbohydrate units per 1 oz (30 g)	Carbohydrate units per portion	Size of average portion
canned	20	85	1	4	4 oz (114 g)
medlars, raw	10	10	½	½	1 large
melon					
cantaloupe	5	40	¼	2	1 medium slice
honeydew	4	25	¼	1	1 medium slice
ogen	3	20	¼	1	½ medium
water	5	50	¼	3	1 large slice
mulberries					
raw	10	40	½	2	4 oz (114 g)
canned	25	100	1	4	4 oz (114 g)
nectarines, raw	15	75	¾	3	1 medium
oranges					
segments	10	40	½	2	4 oz (114 g)
whole	5	40	¼	2	1 large
juice, fresh	10	50	½	2½	¼ pt (142 ml)
canned, no sugar	10	100	½	5	¼ pt (142 ml)
canned + sugar	15	75	¾	5½	¼ pt (142 ml)
passion fruit, raw	10	40	½	1½	4 oz (114 g)
paw-paw, canned	20	75	1	4	4 oz (114 g)
peaches					
fresh, raw	10	35	½	2	1 large
dried, raw	60	60	3	3	1 oz (30 g)
stewed, no sugar	20	90	1	4	4 oz (114 g)
stewed + sugar	25	105	1½	5	4 oz (114 g)

	Calories per 1 oz (30 g)	Calories per portion	Carbohydrate units per 1 oz (30 g)	Carbohydrate units per portion	Size of average portion
canned	25	100	1½	4	4 oz (114 g)
pears					
eating	10	45	½	2	1 small
cooking, raw	10	40	½	2	1 small
stewed, no sugar	10	35	½	2	4 oz (114 g)
stewed + sugar	20	75	1	4	4 oz (114 g)
canned	20	90	1	4	4 oz (114 g)
pineapple					
fresh	15	55	¾	3	4 oz (114 g)
canned	20	90	1	4	4 oz (114 g)
juice, canned	15	75	¾	4	¼ pt (142 ml)
plums					
eating	10	10	½	½	1 medium
cooking, raw	5	25	½	1	4 oz (114 g)
stewed, no sugar	5	25	¼	1	4 oz (114 g)
stewed + sugar	15	65	1	4	4 oz (114 g)
pomegranate					
raw	10	75	¾	4	1 fruit
juice, no sugar	15	60	½	3	¼ pt (142 ml)
prunes					
dried, raw	40	40	2	2	1 oz (30 g)
stewed, no sugar	25	95	1	4	4 oz (114 g)
stewed + sugar	30	120	1½	6	4 oz (114 g)
canned	25	100	1½	6	4 oz (114 g)
raisins, dried	70	70	3½	3½	1 oz (30 g)

	Calories per 1 oz (30 g)	Calories per portion	Carbohydrate units per 1 oz (30 g)	Carbohydrate units per portion	Size of average portion
raspberries					
raw	5	25	¼	I	4 oz (114 g)
stewed, no sugar	5	25	¼	I	4 oz (114 g)
stewed + sugar	20	80	I	4	4 oz (114 g)
canned	25	100	I	5	4 oz (114 g)
redcurrants					
raw	5	25	¼	I	4 oz (114 g)
stewed, no sugar	5	20	¼	I	4 oz (114 g)
stewed + sugar	15	60	¾	3	4 oz (114 g)
rhubarb					
raw	2	10	0	0	5 oz (142 g)
stewed, no sugar	2	10	0	0	5 oz (142 g)
stewed + sugar	15	60	¾	3	5 oz (142 g)
canned	15	75	½	3	5 oz (142 g)
satsuma	5	20	0	I	I medium
strawberries					
raw	10	45	¼	2	6 oz (171 g)
canned	25	125	I	5	5 oz (142 g)
sultanas	70	70	3½	3½	I oz (30 g)
tangerine	5	20	¼	I	I medium
canned	15	60	I	3	4 oz (114 g)
white currants					
raw	5	30	¼	I	4 oz (114 g)
stewed, no sugar	5	25	¼	I	4 oz (114 g)
stewed + sugar	15	60	I	3	4 oz (114 g)

	Calories per 1 oz (30 g)	Calories per portion	Carbohydrate units per 1 oz (30 g)	Carbohydrate units per portion	Size of average portion
fruit cakes					
rich	95	280	3	9	3 oz (85 g)
iced	100	300	3½	10	3 oz (85 g)
plain	100	300	3	9	3 oz (85 g)
fruit gums	50	50	2½	2½	1 oz (30 g)
fruit salad, canned	25	110	1½	6	4 oz (114 g)
fruit shortcake biscuit	150	50	4½	1½	1 biscuit

garlic	5	1	0	0	1 clove
gelatine	95	15	0	0	1 tsp
ginger ale	10	30	½	2	4 oz (114 ml)
gingerbread	105	315	3½	10	3 oz (85 g)
gingernuts	130	65	4½	2	1 biscuit
glacé cherry	60	10	3	½	1 cherry
glucose	110	20	6	1	1 tsp
glucose drink	20	200	1	10	½ pt (284 ml)

	Calories per 1 oz (30 g)	Calories per portion	Carbohydrate units per 1 oz (30 g)	Carbohydrate units per portion	Size of average portion
golden syrup	85	85	4½	4½	1 tbsp
goose					
raw	65	65	0	0	1 oz (30 g)
roast	90	360	0	0	4 oz (114 g)
gooseberries					
green, raw	5	20	0	¾	4 oz (114 g)
stewed, no sugar	4	15	0	¾	4 oz (114 g)
stewed + sugar	15	55	¾	3	4 oz (114 g)
ripe, raw	10	40	½	2	4 oz (114 g)
canned	40	120	2	8	4 oz (114 g)
grape juice	20	100	1	4½	¼ pt (142 ml)
grapefruit					
fresh	3	15	¼	2	½ medium
canned	15	65	1	3½	4 oz (114 g)
grapefruit juice					
no sugar	10	50	½	2	¼ pt (142 ml)
+ sugar	10	55	½	3	¼ pt (142 ml)
grapenuts	100	100	4½	4½	1 oz (30 g)
grapes					
black or white, raw	20	70	1	4	4 oz (114 g)
gravy browning	80	20	1	0	1 tsp
greengages					
raw	15	15	1	1	1 fruit
stewed, no sugar	10	45	½	2	4 oz (114 g)
stewed + sugar	20	85	1	4	4 oz (114 g)
grissini	85	15	3½	1	1 stick

	Calories per 1 oz (30 g)	Calories per portion	Carbohydrate units per 1 oz (30 g)	Carbohydrate units per portion	Size of average portion
grouse, roast	50	300	0	0	1 small
gruyère cheese	130	130	0	0	1 oz (30 g)
guava, canned	15	60	1	4	4 oz (114 g)

haddock					
fresh raw	20	20	0	0	1 oz (30 g)
fresh fried	50	250	0	0	5 oz (142 g)
fresh steamed	30	150	0	0	5 oz (142 g)
smoked, raw	20	20	0	0	1 oz (30 g)
smoked, steamed	30	145	0	0	5 oz (142 g)
haggis boiled	90	525	1	6	6 oz (171 g)
hake					
raw	20	20	0	0	1 oz (30 g)
poached	30	150	0	0	5 oz (142 g)

	Calories per 1 oz (30 g)	Calories per portion	Carbohydrate units per 1 oz (30 g)	Carbohydrate units per portion	Size of average portion
halibut					
raw	25	25	0	0	1 oz (30 g)
steamed	35	185	0	0	5 oz (142 g)
poached	40	190	0	0	5 oz (142 g)
fried	50	240	0	0	5 oz (142 g)
ham					
boiled	75	230	0	0	3 oz (85 g)
smoked	60	190	0	0	3 oz (85 g)
canned	35	105	0	0	3 oz (85 g)
prosciutto	65	65	0	0	1 oz (30 g)
parma	65	65	0	0	1 oz (85 g)
ham & pork canned	75	230	0	0	3 oz (85 g)
hare					
raw	40	40	0	0	1 oz (30 g)
roast	55	215	0	0	4 oz (114 g)
stewed	55	320	0	0	6 oz (171 g)
haricot beans					
boiled	25	100	1	4	4 oz (114 g)
hazel nuts	110	110	¼	¼	1 oz (30 g)
heart					
lamb, raw	35	35	0	0	1 oz (30 g)
sheep, roast	65	270	0	0	4 oz (114 g)
ox, stewed	50	300	0	0	6 oz (171 g)
herring					
raw	65	65	0	0	1 oz (30 g)
steamed	55	280	0	0	5 oz (142 g)

Herring

	Calories per 1 oz (30 g)	Calories per portion	Carbohydrate units per 1 oz (30 g)	Carbohydrate units per portion	Size of average portion
fried in oatmeal	65	330	0	0	5 oz (142 g)
pickled	80	160	0	0	2 oz (57 g)
roe, fried	70	140	¼	½	2 oz (57 g)
high protein cornflakes	110	55	4½	2	½ oz (14 g)
honey comb	80	160	4	8	2 oz (57 g)
in jars (clear & thick)	80	15	4	¾	1 tsp
horseradish raw	15	15	½	½	1 oz (30 g)
sauce	60	30	1½	¾	1 dsp
hot cross bun	80	310	2½	10	1 bun
hot pot	30	320	½	6	10 oz (284 g)
houmous	100	200	¼	½	2 oz (57 g)
hovis bread	65	65	2½	2½	1 oz (30 g)

I

	Calories per 1 oz (30 g)	Calories per portion	Carbohydrate units per 1 oz (30 g)	Carbohydrate units per portion	Size of average portion
ice cream					
dairy, Cornish	45	95	1½	3	2 oz (57 g)
non-dairy	45	90	1	2	2 oz (57 g)
cassata	45	95	1½	3	2 oz (57 g)
chocolate	45	95	1½	3	2 oz (57 g)
pistachio	55	110	1½	3	2 oz (57 g)
strawberry	45	95	1½	3	2 oz (57 g)
ice cream cone	75	25	15	5	1 cone
ice cream wafer	75	10	15	3	1 wafer
instant porridge	110	110	4	4	1 oz (30 g)
instant whip	30	150	1	4½	5 oz (142 g)
Irish coffee	40	200	1	5	¼ pt (142 ml)
Irish stew	35	530	½	9	15 oz (426 g)
jam, all kinds	75	20	4	1	1 tsp
jam tart	120	120	3½	3½	1 tart

	Calories per 1 oz (30 g)	Calories per portion	Carbohydrate units per 1 oz (30 g)	Carbohydrate units per portion	Size of average portion
jellied eel	60	230	0	0	4 oz (114 g)
jellied veal	35	140	0	0	4 oz (114 g)
jelly					
made + water	15	70	¾	3	4 oz (114 g)
made + milk	25	100	1	4	4 oz (114 g)
jelly cubes	75	75	3½	3½	1 oz (30 g)
Jerusalem artichokes, boiled	5	20	¼	1	4 oz (114 g)
kedgeree	45	300	½	3½	7 oz (199 g)
keg bitter	10	100	½	5	½ oz (284 g)
kidney					
lamb, raw	25	25	0	0	1 oz (30 g)
lamb, fried	45	180	0	0	4 oz (114 g)
ox, raw	25	25	0	0	1 oz (30 g)
ox, stewed	50	295	0	0	6 oz (171 g)
pig, raw	25	25	0	0	1 oz (30 g)
pig, stewed	45	260	0	0	6 oz (171 g)
kipper					
raw	80	80	0	0	1 oz (30 g)
baked	60	290	0	0	5 oz (142 g)
fried	70	340	0	0	5 oz (142 g)
kirsch	65	65	3	3	1 oz (30 ml)
kohlrabi					
raw	5	5	0	0	1 oz (30 ml)
boiled	3	15	0	0	5 oz (142 g)

	Calories per 1 oz (30 g)	Calories per portion	Carbohydrate units per 1 oz (30 g)	Carbohydrate units per portion	Size of average portion
ladies' fingers					
raw	5	5	0	0	I oz (30 g)
boiled	5	20	0	½	4 oz (114 g)
canned	5	20	0	½	4 oz (114 g)
lager					
bottled	10	100	½	3	½ pt (284 ml)
draught	10	100	½	3	½ pt (284 ml)
lamb					
lean, raw	45	45	0	0	I oz (30 g)
fat, raw	190	190	0	0	I oz (30 g)
breast, raw	110	110	0	0	I oz (30 g)
breast, roast	115	470	0	0	4 oz (114 g)
chop, raw	105	105	0	0	I oz (30 g)
chop, grilled	100	400	0	0	4 oz (114 g)
cutlet, raw	110	110	0	0	I oz (30 g)
cutlet, grilled	105	210	0	0	I cutlet

	Calories per 1 oz (30 g)	Calories per portion	Carbohydrate units per 1 oz (30 g)	Carbohydrate units per portion	Size of average portion
leg, raw	70	70	0	0	1 oz (30 g)
leg, roast	75	300	0	0	4 oz (114 g)
scrag & neck, raw	90	90	0	0	1 oz (30 g)
scrag & neck, stewed	85	345	0	0	5 oz (142 g)
shoulder, raw	90	90	0	0	1 oz (30 g)
shoulder, roast	90	360	0	0	4 oz (114 g)
lancashire cheese	100	100	0	0	1 oz (30 g)
lard	255	255	0	0	1 oz (30 g)
lardy cake	105	410	3½	14½	4 oz (114 g)
laverbread	15	15	0	0	1 oz (30 g)
leeks					
raw	10	10	0	0	1 oz (30 g)
boiled	5	30	0	0	4 oz (114 g)
leicester cheese	110	110	0	0	1 oz (30 g)
lemons, whole	5	15	¼	½	1 medium
lemon curd	80	15	3½	½	1 tsp
homemade	80	15	2	¼	1 tsp
lemon juice, fresh	2	2	0	0	1 oz (30 ml)
lemon meringue pie	90	370	2½	10	4 oz (114 g)
lemon mousse, frozen	40	110	1	2½	3½ oz (110 g)
lemon sole					
raw	25	25	0	0	1 oz (30 g)
steamed	25	130	0	0	5 oz (142 g)
fried in breadcrumbs	60	310	0	½	5 oz (142 g)

	Calories per 1 oz (30 g)	Calories per portion	Carbohydrate units per 1 oz (30 g)	Carbohydrate units per portion	Size of average portion
lemon sponge	145	170	5½	6	1 small piece
lemon squash, undiluted	30	30	1½	1½	1 oz (30 ml)
lemonade, bottled	5	60	¼	3	½ pt (284 ml)
lentils					
raw	85	85	3	3	1 oz (30 g)
split or whole, boiled	30	120	1	4	4 oz (114 g)
dahl masur	25	105	¾	1½	4 oz (114 g)
lentil soup	30	300	¾	6	½ pt (284 ml)
lettuce raw	3	10	0	0	3 oz (85 g)
lime juice, undiluted	30	30	1½	1½	1 oz (30 ml)
liquorice all sorts	90	350	4	16	4 oz (114 g)
liver					
calf, raw	45	45	0	0	1 oz (30 g)
calf, fried	70	290	0	0	4 oz (114 g)
chicken, raw	40	40	0	0	1 oz (30 g)
chicken, fried	55	220	0	1	4 oz (114 g)
lamb, raw	50	50	0	0	1 oz (30 g)
lamb, fried	65	260	¼	1	4 oz (114 g)
ox, raw	45	45	0	0	1 oz (30 g)
ox, stewed	55	335	¼	1	6 oz (171 g)
pig, raw	45	45	0	0	1 oz (30 g)
pig, stewed	55	320	¼	1	6 oz (171 g)
liver sausage	90	180	¼	½	2 oz (57 g)
lobster boiled	35	175	0	0	5 oz (142 g)

	Calories per 1 oz (30 g)	Calories per portion	Carbohydrate units per 1 oz (30 g)	Carbohydrate units per portion	Size of average portion
loganberries					
raw	5	20	¼	1	4 oz (114 g)
stewed, no sugar	5	20	¼	1	4 oz (114 g)
stewed + sugar	15	60	¾	3	4 oz (114 g)
canned	30	110	1½	6	4 oz (114 g)
low fat spread	105	20	0	0	1 tsp
luncheon meat, canned	90	270	¼	1	3 oz (85 g)
lychee					
raw	20	20	1	1	1 oz (30 g)
canned	20	80	1	4	4 oz (114 g)

macaroni					
raw	105	105	4½	4½	1 oz (30 g)
boiled	35	350	1½	14	10 oz (284 g)
macaroni cheese	50	500	1	10	10 oz (284 g)
macaroon	100	200	2½	5	1 large

	Calories per 1 oz (30 g)	Calories per portion	Carbohydrate units per 1 oz (30 g)	Carbohydrate units per portion	Size of average portion
mackerel					
raw	65	65	0	0	1 oz (30 g)
fried	55	275	0	0	5 oz (142 g)
steamed	75	380	0	0	5 oz (142 g)
smoked	90	440	0	0	5 oz (142 g)
madeira	35	35	1½	1½	1 oz (30 ml)
madeira cake	110	330	3½	10	3 oz (85 g)
maize oil	255	255	0	0	1 oz (30 ml)
malt bread	70	70	3	3	1 oz (30 g)
malted milk powder	115	40	4	1	2 tsp
mandarin					
raw	10	25	½	1	1 small
canned	15	160	1	4	4 oz (114 g)
mango					
raw	15	105	1	6	1 medium
canned	20	85	1	4	4 oz (114 g)
margarine	210	50	0	0	1 tsp
marmalade	75	20	4	1	1 tsp
marrow					
raw	3	3	0	0	1 oz (30 g)
boiled	1	5	0	0	4 oz (114 g)
marshmallow	95	95	4½	4½	1 oz (30 g)
marzipan	125	125	3	3	1 oz (30 g)
matzo biscuit	110	110	5	5	1 oz (30 g)
mayonnaise, homemade	205	100	0	0	1 dsp

	Calories per 1 oz (30 g)	Calories per portion	Carbohydrate units per 1 oz (30 g)	Carbohydrate units per portion	Size of average portion
MEAT					
bacon gammon joint					
raw	65	65	0	0	1 oz (30 g)
boiled	75	300	0	0	4 oz (114 g)
bacon gammon rashers, grilled	65	260	0	0	4 oz (114 g)
bacon rashers, raw					
back	120	360	0	0	2 rashers
middle	120	360	0	0	2 rashers
streaky	120	240	0	0	2 rashers
bacon rashers, fried					
back	130	260	0	0	2 rashers
middle	135	270	0	0	2 rashers
streaky	140	210	0	0	2 rashers
bacon rashers, grilled					
back	115	160	0	0	2 rashers
middle	120	190	0	0	2 rashers
streaky	120	130	0	0	2 rashers
beef					
lean, raw	35	35	0	0	1 oz (30 g)
fat, raw	180	180	0	0	1 oz (30 g)
brisket, boiled	90	380	0	0	4 oz (114 g)
forerib, roast	100	400	0	0	4 oz (114 g)
beef joint					
roast	100	400	0	0	4 oz (114 g)
corned	60	120	0	0	2 oz (57 g)

	Calories per 1 oz (30 g)	Calories per portion	Carbohydrate units per 1 oz (30 g)	Carbohydrate units per portion	Size of average portion
beef minced					
lean, raw	35	35	0	0	1 oz (30 g)
fat, raw	65	65	0	0	1 oz (30 g)
stewed	65	260	0	0	4 oz (114 g)
beef silverside					
boiled	70	280	0	0	4 oz (114 g)
boiled, lean only	50	200	0	0	4 oz (114 g)
beef, sirloin roast	80	240	0	0	3 oz (85 g)
beef steak					
raw	55	55	0	0	1 oz (30 g)
grilled	55	330	0	0	6 oz (171 g) raw
fried	65	390	0	0	6 oz (171 g) raw
beef stewing steak					
raw	50	50	0	0	1 oz (30 g)
stewed	65	260	0	0	4 oz (114 g)
frogs' legs					
raw	20	20	0	0	1 oz (30 g)
fried in batter	85	255	0	0	12 legs
lamb					
lean, raw	45	45	0	0	1 oz (30 g)
fat, raw	190	190	0	0	1 oz (30 g)
breast, raw	110	110	0	0	1 oz (30 g)
breast, roast	115	470	0	0	4 oz (114 g)
chop, raw	105	105	0	0	1 oz (30 g)
chop, grilled	100	400	0	0	4 oz (114 g)
cutlet, raw	110	110	0	0	1 oz (30 g)

	Calories per 1 oz (30 g)	Calories per portion	Carbohydrate units per 1 oz (30 g)	Carbohydrate units per portion	Size of average portion
cutlet, grilled	105	210	0	0	4 oz (114 g)
leg, raw	70	70	0	0	1 oz (30 g)
leg roast	75	300	0	0	4 oz (114 g)
scag & neck, raw	90	90	0	0	1 oz (30 g)
scrag & neck, stewed	85	345	0	0	5 oz (142 g)
shoulder, raw	90	90	0	0	1 oz (30 g)
shoulder, roast	90	360	0	0	4 oz (114 g)
pork					
lean, raw	40	40	0	0	1 oz (30 g)
fat, raw	190	190	0	0	1 oz (30 g)
belly rashers, raw	110	110	0	0	1 oz (30 g)
belly rashers, grilled	115	450	0	0	4 oz (114 g)
chop, raw	95	95	0	0	1 oz (30 g)
chop, grilled	95	565	0	0	1 chop
ham					
boiled	75	230	0	0	3 oz (85 g)
smoked	60	190	0	0	3 oz (85 g)
canned	35	105	0	0	3 oz (85 g)
prosciutto	65	65	0	0	1 oz (30 g)
parma	65	65	0	0	1 oz (30 g)
leg, raw	75	75	0	0	1 oz (30 g)
leg, roast	80	325	0	0	4 oz (114 g)
snails with butter	180	270	0	0	6 snails
veal					
cutlet, fried	60	365	¼	1½	1 cutlet
fillet, raw	30	30	0	0	1 oz (30 g)

	Calories per 1 oz (30 g)	Calories per portion	Carbohydrate units per 1 oz (30 g)	Carbohydrate units per portion	Size of average portion
fillet, roast	65	260	0	0	4 oz (114 g)
jellied	35	140	0	0	4 oz (114 g)

MEAT PRODUCTS

beefburgers					
fried	75	300	0	0	1 average
grilled	75	290	0	1	1 average
beef steak pudding	65	390	1	6	6 oz (171 g)
beef stew	35	210	¼	1	6 oz (171 g)
black pudding	85	170	1	2	2 oz (57 g)
bolognese sauce	40	240	¼	1	6 oz (171 g)
brawn	45	90	0	0	2 oz (57 g)
cornish pasty	95	570	2	11	6 oz (171 g)
curried meat	45	270	½	2½	6 oz (171 g)
faggots	75	600	¾	7	2 faggots
frankfurters	80	80	¼	¼	1 small
haggis boiled	90	525	0	0	6 oz (171 g)
hot pot	30	320	½	6	10 oz (284 g)
Irish stew	35	530	½	6	15 oz (426 g)
luncheon meat canned	90	270	¼	1	3 oz (85 g)
meat paste	50	10	0	0	1 tsp
mortadella	85	285	0	0	3 oz (85 g)
moussaka	55	550	½	5	10 oz (284 g)
pâté (chicken liver, duck & game)	95	95	0	0	1 oz (30 g)

83

	Calories per 1 oz (30 g)	Calories per portion	Carbohydrate units per 1 oz (30 g)	Carbohydrate units per portion	Size of average portion
pâté goose liver	110	110	0	0	1 oz (30 g)
polony	80	160	1	2	2 oz (57 g)
salami	140	280	0	0	2 oz (57 g)
sausages					
beef, fried	75	150	½	1	1 sausage
beef, grilled	55	110	½	1	1 sausage
pork, fried	90	180	½	1	1 sausage
pork, grilled	90	125	¾	1	1 sausage
sausage roll					
flaky pastry	135	270	2	4	1 small
short pastry	110	220	2	4	1 small
saveloy	75	150	½	1	2 oz (57 g)
shepherd's pie	35	350	½	5	10 oz (284 g)
steak & kidney pie					
single crust	80	640	1	8	8 oz (227 g)
individual	90	735	1½	11	8 oz (227 g)
stewed steak with gravy	50	400	0	0	8 oz (227 g)
white pudding	130	255	2	4	2 oz (57 g)
medlars, raw	10	10	½	½	1 large
melons					
cantaloupe	5	40	¼	2	1 medium slice
honeydew	4	25	¼	1	1 medium slice
ogen	3	20	¼	1	½ medium
water	5	50	¼	3	1 large slice

	Calories per 1 oz (30 g)	Calories per portion	Carbohydrate units per 1 oz (30 g)	Carbohydrate units per portion	Size of average portion
meringue	110	50	5½	2½	1 large
milk, cows					
whole	20	20	¼	¼	1 oz (30 ml)
sterilized	20	20	¼	¼	1 oz (30 ml)
long life	20	20	¼	¼	1 oz (30 ml)
skimmed	10	10	¼	¼	1 oz (30 ml)
semi-skimmed (light)	15	15	¼	¼	1 oz (30 ml)
condensed, whole, sweetened	90	90	3	3	1 oz (30 ml)
skimmed, sweetened	75	75	3½	3½	1 oz (30 ml)
evaporated, whole, unsweetened	45	45	¾	¾	1 oz (30 ml)
dried, whole	140	35	2	½	2 tsp
dried, skimmed	100	15	3	½	2 tsp
milk, goats	20	20	¼	¼	1 oz (30 ml)
milk jelly	25	100	1	4	4 oz (114 g)
milk pudding	35	220	1	6	6 oz (171 g)
canned rice	25	150	¾	5	6 oz (171 g)
mince pies	125	210	3½	6	1 pie
mincemeat	65	65	3½	3½	1 oz (30 g)
minerals					
bitter lemon	10	40	½	2	4 oz (114 ml)
ginger ale	10	30	½	2	4 oz (114 ml)
soda water	0	0	0	0	4 oz (114 ml)
tonic water	5	20	¼	1	4 oz (114 ml)
minestrone soup	5	65	¼	2	½ pt (284 ml)

	Calories per 1 oz (30 g)	Calories per portion	Carbohydrate units per 1 oz (30 g)	Carbohydrate units per portion	Size of average portion
mint sauce (in jars, undiluted)	30	30	1½	1½	1 oz (30 g)
mortadella	85	285	0	0	3 oz (85 g)
moussaka	55	550	½	5	10 oz (284 g)
mousse, frozen					
chocolate	35	100	1	3	3½ oz (110 g)
fruit	40	110	1	2½	3½ oz (100 g)
mozzarella cheese	95	95	0	0	1 oz (30 g)
muesli	105	210	4	8	2 oz (57 g)
muffin	65	130	3	5½	1 muffin
mulberries					
raw	10	40	½	2	4 oz (114 g)
canned	25	100	1	4	4 oz (114 g)
mullet					
raw	40	40	0	0	1 oz (30 g)
steamed	50	250	0	0	5 oz (142 g)
fried	60	300	0	0	5 oz (142 g)
mulligatawny soup	10	100	½	3	½ pt (284 ml)
mung beans					
raw	65	65	2	2	1 oz (30 g)
cooked dahl	30	60	¾	1½	2 oz (57 g)
mushrooms					
raw	4	4	0	0	1 oz (30 g)
boiled	2	5	0	0	2 oz (57 g)
fried	60	120	0	0	2 oz (57 g)
soup, canned	15	150	¼	2	½ pt (284 ml)

	Calories per 1 oz (30 g)	Calories per portion	Carbohydrate units per 1 oz (30 g)	Carbohydrate units per portion	Size of average portion
mussels					
raw	20	20	0	0	1 oz (30 g)
steamed	25	75	0	0	3 oz (85 g)
canned	20	55	0	0	3 oz (85 g)
mustard powder	130	15	1	0	1 tsp
mustard & cress	3	3	0	0	1 oz (30 g)

nectarines, raw	15	45	¾	2	1 medium
NUTS					
almonds	160	320	¼	½	2 oz (57 g)
Brazil nuts	175	350	¼	½	2 oz (57 g)
cashew nuts	155	610	1	3½	4 oz (114 g)
chestnuts	50	100	2	4	2 oz (57 g)
hazelnuts	110	110	¼	¼	1 oz (30 g)

	Calories per 1 oz (30 g)	Calories per portion	Carbohydrate units per 1 oz (30 g)	Carbohydrate units per portion	Size of average portion
peanuts, fresh or dry roasted or roasted and salted	160	160	½	½	1 oz (30 g)
pistachio nuts, shelled, raw	170	170	1	1	1 oz (30 g)
walnuts, shelled	150	150	¼	¼	1 oz (30 g)

oatcakes	125	60	3½	2	1 biscuit
oatmeal, raw	115	115	4	4	1 oz (30 g)
octopus					
raw	20	20	0	0	1 oz (30 g)
steamed	25	125	0	0	5 oz (142 g)
fried	30	160	0	0	5 oz (142 g)
fried in batter	55	340	½	2½	5 oz (142 g)

	Calories per 1 oz (30 g)	Calories per portion	Carbohydrate units per 1 oz (30 g)	Carbohydrate units per portion	Size of average portion
OFFAL					
brain					
calf, boiled	45	135	0	0	3 oz (85 g)
lamb, boiled	35	105	0	0	3 oz (85 g)
heart					
lamb, raw	35	35	0	0	1 oz (30 g)
sheep, roast	65	270	0	0	4 oz (114 g)
ox, raw	30	30	0	0	1 oz (30 g)
ox, stewed	50	300	0	0	6 oz (171 g)
kidney					
lamb, raw	25	25	0	0	1 oz (30 g)
lamb, fried	45	180	0	0	4 oz (114 g)
ox, raw	25	25	0	0	1 oz (30 g)
ox, stewed	50	295	0	0	6 oz (171 g)
pig, raw	25	25	0	0	1 oz (30 g)
pig, stewed	45	260	0	0	6 oz (171 g)
liver					
calf, raw	45	45	0	0	1 oz (30 g)
calf, fried	70	290	0	0	4 oz (114 g)
chicken, raw	40	40	0	0	1 oz (30 g)
chicken, fried	55	220	0	1	4 oz (114 g)
lamb, raw	50	50	0	0	1 oz (30 g)
lamb, fried	65	260	¼	1	4 oz (114 g)
ox, raw	45	45	0	0	1 oz (30 g)
ox, stewed	55	335	¼	1	6 oz (171 g)
pig, raw	45	45	0	0	1 oz (30 g)

	Calories per 1 oz (30 g)	Calories per portion	Carbohydrate units per 1 oz (30 g)	Carbohydrate units per portion	Size of average portion
pig, stewed	55	320	¼	1	6 oz (171 g)
oxtail					
raw	50	50	0	0	1 oz (30 g)
stewed	70	515	¼	2	8 oz (227 g)
sweetbread					
lamb, raw	35	35	0	0	1 oz (30 g)
lamb, fried	65	260	¼	1	4 oz (114 g)
tongue					
lamb, raw	55	55	0	0	1 oz (30 g)
sheep, stewed	80	490	0	0	6 oz (171 g)
ox, pickled	60	60	0	0	1 oz (30 g)
ox, pickled and boiled	85	170	0	0	2 oz (57 g)
canned	60	120	0	0	2 oz (57 g)
tripe					
dressed	15	15	0	0	1 oz (30 g)
stewed	30	180	0	0	6 oz (171 g)
okra					
raw	5	5	0	0	1 oz (30 g)
boiled	5	20	0	0	4 oz (114 g)
canned	5	20	0	0	4 oz (114 g)
olives					
black or green	25	25	0	0	10 olives
stuffed	30	30	0	0	10 olives
olive oil	255	255	0	0	1 oz (30 ml)
omelette, plain	55	275	0	0	5 oz (142 g)

	Calories per 1 oz (30 g)	Calories per portion	Carbohydrate units per 1 oz (30 g)	Carbohydrate units per portion	Size of average portion
onions					
raw	5	5	0	0	1 oz (30 g)
boiled	4	15	0	0	4 oz (114 g)
fried	100	100	½	½	1 oz (30 g)
pickled	5	5	0	0	1 oz (30 g)
spring, raw	10	3	0	0	1 onion
onion sauce	30	90	½	1½	3 oz (85 g)
oranges					
segments	10	40	½	2	4 oz (114 g)
whole	5	40	¼	2	1 large
orange juice fresh or canned, no sugar	10	50	½	2½	¼ pt (142 ml)
canned + sugar	15	75	¾	5½	¼ pt (142 ml)
orange marmalade	75	20	4	1	1 tsp
orange squash, undiluted	30	30	1½	1½	1 oz (30 ml)
ouzo	65	65	3	3	1 oz (30 ml)
oxtail					
raw	50	50	0	0	1 oz (30 g)
stewed	70	515	¼	2	8 oz (227 g)
oxtail soup	15	150	0	2	½ pt (284 ml)
oysters					
raw	15	15	0	0	2 oysters
canned	15	45	0	0	6 oysters
smoked	15	45	0	0	3 oz (85 g)

	Calories per 1 oz (30 g)	Calories per portion	Carbohydrate units per 1 oz (30 g)	Carbohydrate units per portion	Size of average portion
pale ale, bottled	10	100	½	5	½ pt (284 ml)
palm heart, canned	30	120	1½	6	4 oz (114 g)
palm oil	255	255	0	0	1 oz (30 ml)
palmier	160	55	3	1	1 biscuit
pancakes	85	85	2	2	1 thin
parma ham	65	65	0	0	1 oz (30 g)
parmesan cheese	120	20	0	0	2 tsp
parsley, raw	5	5	0	0	1 oz (30 g)
parsnips, boiled	15	60	¾	3	4 oz (114 g)
partridge, roast	60	240	0	0	4 oz (114 g)
passion fruit, raw	10	40	½	1½	4 oz (114 g)
pasty, Cornish	95	570	2	11	6 oz (171 g)
pastis	70	70	3	3	1 oz (30 ml)
pastilles, fruit	70	70	3½	3½	1 oz (30 g)
pastry, choux					
raw	60	60	1	1	1 oz (30 g)
cooked	95	95	1½	1½	1 oz (30 g)

	Calories per 1 oz (30 g)	Calories per portion	Carbohydrate units per 1 oz (30 g)	Carbohydrate units per portion	Size of average portion
pastry, flaky					
raw	120	120	2	2	1 oz (30 g)
cooked	160	160	2½	2½	1 oz (30 g)
pastry, short					
raw	130	130	2½	2½	1 oz (30 g)
cooked	150	150	3	3	1 oz (30 g)
pâté, chicken liver, duck & game	95	95	0	0	1 oz (30 g)
pâté, goose liver	110	110	0	0	1 oz (30 g)
paw-paw, canned	20	75	1	4	4 oz (114 g)
peaches					
fresh, raw	10	35	½	2	1 large
dried, raw	60	60	3	3	1 oz (30 g)
stewed, no sugar	10	35	½	2	4 oz (114 g)
stewed + sugar	20	75	1	4	4 oz (114 g)
canned	20	90	1	4	4 oz (114 g)
peach jam	75	20	4	1	1 tsp
peanuts, fresh or dry roasted & salted	160	160	½	½	1 oz (30 g)
peanut brittle	120	120	4	4	1 oz (30 g)
peanut butter	175	175	¾	¾	1 oz (30 g)
peanut oil	255	255	0	0	1 oz (30 ml)
pears					
eating	10	45	½	2	1 small
cooking, raw	10	40	½	2	1 small
stewed, no sugar	10	35	½	2	4 oz (114 g)

	Calories per 1 oz (30 g)	Calories per portion	Carbohydrate units per 1 oz (30 g)	Carbohydrate units per portion	Size of average portion
stewed + sugar	20	75	I	4	4 oz (114 g)
canned	20	90	I	4	4 oz (114 g)
pears, avocado	65	250	0	½	½ large
pearl barley					
raw	100	100	5	5	I oz (30 g)
boiled	35	35	2	2	I oz (30 g)
peas					
fresh, raw	20	20	½	½	I oz (30 g)
fresh, boiled	15	45	½	I	3 oz (85 g)
frozen, raw	15	15	½	½	I oz (30 g)
frozen, boiled	10	30	¼	I	3 oz (85 g)
canned, garden	15	45	½	I	3 oz (85 g)
canned, processed	25	65	¾	3	3 oz (85 g)
dried, raw	80	80	3	3	I oz (30 g)
dried, boiled	30	90	I	3	3 oz (85 g)
split, raw	90	90	3	3	I oz (30 g)
split, boiled	35	105	I	4	3 oz (85 g)
chick, raw	90	90	3	3	I oz (30 g)
chick, cooked dahl	40	160	I	4	4 oz (114 g)
red pigeon, raw	85	85	3	3	I oz (30 g)
red pigeon, cooked	30	90	I	3	3 oz (85 g)
peppers					
raw	4	10	0	0	2 oz (57 g)
boiled	4	10	0	0	2 oz (57 g)
peppermint creams, chocolate coated	120	120	4	4	I oz (30 g)

	Calories per 1 oz (30 g)	Calories per portion	Carbohydrate units per 1 oz (30 g)	Carbohydrate units per portion	Size of average portion
peppermints	110	110	6	6	1 oz (30 g)
pheasant, roast	60	240	0	0	4 oz (114 g)
piccalilli	10	10	¼	¼	1 oz (30 g)
pickle, sweet	40	40	2	2	1 oz (30 g)
pickled onions	5	5	0	0	1 oz (30 g)
pie					
apple	50	300	1½	7½	6 oz (171 g)
fish	35	280	¼	6	8 oz (227 g)
gooseberry	50	300	1½	7½	6 oz (171 g)
lemon meringue	90	370	2½	10	4 oz (114 g)
mince	125	210	3½	6	1 pie
plum	50	300	1½	7½	6 oz (171 g)
pork	105	420	1½	6	4 oz (114 g)
rhubarb	50	300	1½	7½	6 oz (171 g)
shepherd's	35	350	½	5	10 oz (284 g)
pigeon, roast	65	260	0	0	4 oz (114 g)
pigeon peas					
raw	85	85	3	3	1 oz (30 g)
cooked	30	90	1	3	3 oz (85 g)
pilchards					
canned in oil	65	250	0	0	4 oz (114 g)
canned in tomato sauce	35	140	0	¼	4 oz (114 g)
pineapple					
fresh	15	55	¾	3	4 oz (114 g)
canned	20	90	1	4	4 oz (114 g)

	Calories per 1 oz (30 g)	Calories per portion	Carbohydrate units per 1 oz (30 g)	Carbohydrate units per portion	Size of average portion
juice, canned	15	75	¾	4	¼ pt (142 ml)
pistachio nuts, shelled raw	170	170	1	1	1 oz (30 g)
pizza, cheese & tomato	65	260	1½	6	1 small
plaice					
raw	25	25	0	0	1 oz (30 g)
steamed	25	130	0	0	5 oz (142 g)
fried in batter	80	400	¾	4	5 oz (142 g)
fried in breadcrumbs	65	325	½	2½	5 oz (142 g)
plantain					
green, boiled	35	140	2	7	4 oz (114 g)
ripe, fried	75	300	2½	7	4 oz (114 g)
plums					
fresh, raw	10	10	½	½	1 medium
cooking, raw	5	25	½	1	4 oz (114 g)
stewed, no sugar	5	25	¼	1	4 oz (114 g)
stewed + sugar	15	65	1	4	4 oz (114 g)
plum jam	75	20	4	1	1 tsp
plum pie	50	300	1½	7½	6 oz (171 g)
polony	80	160	1	2	2 oz (57 g)
pomegranate					
raw	10	75	¾	4	1 fruit
juice, no sugar	15	60	½	3	¼ pt (142 ml)
popadom, grilled	100	100	4	4	3 popadoms
popcorn					
plain	110	110	4	4	1 oz (30 g)

	Calories per 1 oz (30 g)	Calories per portion	Carbohydrate units per 1 oz (30 g)	Carbohydrate units per portion	Size of average portion
+ oil & salt	130	130	3	3	1 oz (30 g)
+ sugar	110	110	5	5	1 oz (30 g)
pork					
lean, raw	40	40	0	0	1 oz (30 g)
fat, raw	190	190	0	0	1 oz (30 g)
belly rashers, raw	110	110	0	0	1 oz (30 g)
belly rashers, grilled	115	450	0	0	4 oz (114 g)
chop, raw	95	95	0	0	1 oz (30 g)
chop, grilled	95	565	0	0	1 chop
leg, raw	75	75	0	0	1 oz (30 g)
leg, roast	80	325	0	0	4 oz (114 g)
pork pie	105	420	1½	6	4 oz (114 g)
pork sausages					
fried	90	180	¾	1	1 sausage
grilled	90	125	¾	1	1 sausage
porridge	15	65	½	2	5 oz (142 g)
port	45	90	2	4	2 oz (57 ml)
port salut cheese	90	90	0	0	1 oz (30 g)
potato crisps all flavours	150	125	3	2½	1 small pkt
potato rings	150	150	3½	3½	1 oz (30 g)
potatoes					
old, boiled	25	100	1	4	4 oz (114 g)
old, mashed	35	140	1	4	4 oz (114 g)
old, baked	30	120	1½	6	1 small
old, roast	45	180	1½	6	2 small

	Calories per 1 oz (30 g)	Calories per portion	Carbohydrate units per 1 oz (30 g)	Carbohydrate units per portion	Size of average portion
chips, fresh	70	430	2	12	6 oz (171 g)
chips, frozen	30	30	1	1	1 oz (30 g)
chips, fried	80	495	2	10	6 oz (171 g)
new, boiled	20	85	1	4	4 oz (114 g)
new, canned	15	60	¾	3	4 oz (114 g)
instant powder	90	90	4	4	1 oz (30 g)
instant, made up	20	80	1	4	4 oz (114 g)

POULTRY AND GAME

chicken					
raw, meat only	35	35	0	0	1 oz (30 g)
raw, meat & skin	65	65	0	0	1 oz (30 g)
chicken boiled					
meat only	50	255	0	0	5 oz (142 g)
light meat	45	230	0	0	5 oz (142 g)
dark meat	60	295	0	0	5 oz (142 g)
chicken roast					
meat only	40	210	0	0	5 oz (142 g)
meat & skin	60	290	0	0	5 oz (142 g)
light meat	40	200	0	0	5 oz (142 g)
dark meat	45	220	0	0	5 oz (142 g)
wing quarter	20	65	0	0	1 medium
leg quarter	25	155	0	0	1 small
duck					
raw, meat only	35	35	0	0	1 oz (30 g)
roast, meat only	55	270	0	0	5 oz (142 g)

	Calories per 1 oz (30 g)	Calories per portion	Carbohydrate units per 1 oz (30 g)	Carbohydrate units per portion	Size of average portion
goose					
raw	65	65	0	0	1 oz (29 g)
roast	90	360	0	0	4 oz (114 g)
grouse, roast	50	300	0	0	1 small
hare					
raw	40	40	0	0	1 oz (30 g)
roast	55	215	0	0	4 oz (114 g)
stewed	55	320	0	0	6 oz (171 g)
partridge, roast	60	240	0	0	4 oz (114 g)
pheasant, roast	60	240	0	0	4 oz (114 g)
pigeon, roast	65	260	0	0	4 oz (114 g)
poussin					
roast or grilled	20	250	0	0	1 bird
fried	30	360	0	0	1 bird
quail					
grilled or roast	20	165	0	0	1 bird
fried	30	430	0	0	1 bird
rabbit					
raw	35	35	0	0	1 oz (30 g)
roast or grilled	45	170	0	0	4 oz (114 g)
stewed	50	300	0	0	6 oz (171 g)
turkey					
raw, meat only	30	30	0	0	1 oz (30 g)
raw, meat & skin	40	40	0	0	1 oz (30 g)
turkey roast					
meat only	40	160	0	0	4 oz (114 g)

	Calories per 1 oz (30 g)	Calories per portion	Carbohydrate units per 1 oz (30 g)	Carbohydrate units per portion	Size of average portion
meat & skin	50	200	0	0	4 oz (114 g)
light meat	35	150	0	0	4 oz (114 g)
dark meat	40	170	0	0	4 oz (114 g)
venison raw	40	40	0	0	1 oz (30 g)
roast	55	220	0	0	4 oz (114 g)
fried	65	250	0	0	4 oz (114 g)
grilled	55	225	0	0	4 oz (114 g)
woodcock, roast	20	160	0	0	1 bird
poussin roast or grilled	20	250	0	0	1 bird
fried	30	360	0	0	1 bird
prawns raw, in shells	10	10	0	0	1 oz (30 g)
raw, shelled	30	60	0	0	2 oz (57 g)
boiled	30	60	0	0	2 oz (57 g)
potted	120	240	0	0	2 oz (57 g)
processed cheese	90	90	0	0	1 oz (30 g)
prosciutto ham	65	65	0	0	1 oz (30 g)
prunes dried, raw	40	40	2	2	1 oz (30 g)
stewed, no sugar	25	95	1	4	4 oz (114 g)
stewed + sugar	30	120	1½	6	4 oz (114 g)
canned	25	100	1½	6	4 oz (114 g)
juice	20	110	1	5	¼ pt (142 ml)

	Calories per 1 oz (30 g)	Calories per portion	Carbohydrate units per 1 oz (30 g)	Carbohydrate units per portion	Size of average portion
puffed wheat	95	95	4	4	1 oz (30 g)
pumpernickel	95	95	3½	3½	1 oz (30 g)
pumpkins					
raw	4	4	0	0	1 oz (30 g)
boiled	2	10	0	0	5 oz (142 g)

quail					
grilled or roast	20	165	0	0	1 bird
fried	30	430	0	0	1 bird
queen of puddings	60	360	2	8	6 oz (171 g)
quiche lorraine	110	440	1	4	small slice
quinces, raw	5	5	¼	¼	1 oz (30 g)

	Calories per 1 oz (30 g)	Calories per portion	Carbohydrate units per 1 oz (30 g)	Carbohydrate units per portion	Size of average portion
rabbit					
raw	35	35	0	0	1 oz (30 g)
grilled or roast	45	170	0	0	4 oz (114 g)
fried or boiled	50	200	0	0	4 oz (114 g)
stewed	50	300	0	0	6 oz (171 g)
radishes, raw	4	4	0	0	1 oz (30 g)
raisins, dried	70	70	3½	3½	1 oz (30 g)
raisin bran	100	100	4½	4½	1 oz (30 g)
raspberries					
raw	5	25	¼	1	4 oz (114 g)
stewed, no sugar	5	25	¼	1	4 oz (114 g)
stewed + sugar	20	80	1	4	4 oz (114 g)
canned	25	100	1	5	4 oz (114 g)
ratatouille	20	170	0	0	10 oz (284 g)
ravioli	70	400	1½	8	6 oz (171 g)
redcurrants					
raw	5	25	¼	1	4 oz (114 g)

	Calories per 1 oz (30 g)	Calories per portion	Carbohydrate units per 1 oz (30 g)	Carbohydrate units per portion	Size of average portion
stewed, no sugar	5	20	¼	1	4 oz (114 g)
stewed + sugar	15	60	¾	3	4 oz (114 g)
jam	75	20	4	1	1 tsp
red kidney beans, cooked	25	100	1	4	4 oz (114 g)
retsina	20	100	1	5	¼ pt (142 ml)
rhubarb raw	2	10	0	0	5 oz (142 g)
stewed, no sugar	2	10	0	0	5 oz (142 g)
stewed + sugar	15	60	¾	3	5 oz (142 g)
canned	15	75	½	3	5 oz (142 g)
rhubarb pie	50	300	1½	7½	6 oz (171 g)
rice white, raw	105	105	5	5	1 oz (30 g)
white, boiled	35	35	1½	1½	1 oz (30 g)
brown, raw	100	100	5	5	1 oz (30 g)
brown, boiled	35	35	1½	1½	1 oz (30 g)
rice pudding	35	220	1	6	6 oz (171 g)
canned	25	150	¾	5	6 oz (171 g)
ricotta cheese	70	70	0	0	1 oz (30 g)
rock bun	105	420	3½	14	1 bun
rock salmon, fried in batter	75	375	½	2	5 oz (142 g)
roe, cod fried	55	110	¾	1½	2 oz (57 g)
smoked	30	30	0	0	1 oz (30 g)

	Calories per 1 oz (30 g)	Calories per portion	Carbohydrate units per 1 oz (30 g)	Carbohydrate units per portion	Size of average portion
roe, herring, fried	70	140	¼	½	2 oz (57 g)
rollmops	70	280	0	0	4 oz (114 g)
rolls					
brown, crusty	80	160	2½	5	1 small
brown, soft	80	160	2½	5	1 small
white, crusty	80	160	3½	7	1 small
white, soft	85	170	3	6	1 small
starch reduced	110	25	2½	½	1 roll
roquefort cheese	100	100	0	0	1 oz (30 g)
rosehip syrup, undiluted	65	10	3½	1	1 tsp
rum, white or dark	65	65	3	3	1 oz (30 ml)
runner beans, boiled	5	20	0	0	4 oz (114 g)

| **safflower oil** | 255 | 255 | 0 | 0 | 1 oz (30 ml) |

	Calories per 1 oz (30 g)	Calories per portion	Carbohydrate units per 1 oz (30 g)	Carbohydrate units per portion	Size of average portion
Saint Paulin cheese	90	90	0	0	1 oz (30 g)
sage derby cheese	110	110	0	0	1 oz (30 g)
sago pudding	35	220	1	6	6 oz (171 g)
salad cream	90	45	1	½	1 dsp
salami	140	280	0	0	2 oz (57 g)
salmon					
raw	50	50	0	0	1 oz (30 g)
steamed	55	280	0	0	5 oz (142 g)
fried	65	330	0	0	5 oz (142 g)
smoked	40	80	0	0	2 oz (57 g)
canned	45	90	0	0	2 oz (57 g)
salmon trout					
raw	50	50	0	0	1 oz (30 g)
poached	55	280	0	0	5 oz (142 g)
salsify					
raw	5	5	0	0	1 oz (30 g)
boiled	5	20	0	0	4 oz (114 g)
sangria	20	100	1	5	¼ pt (142 ml)
sardines					
canned in oil drained	60	120	0	0	2 oz (57 g)
canned in tomato sauce	50	100	0	0	2 oz (57 g)
satsumas	5	20	0	1	1 medium
sauces					
bechamel	40	160	½	2	4 oz (114 g)

Sauces

	Calories per 1 oz (30 g)	Calories per portion	Carbohydrate units per 1 oz (30 g)	Carbohydrate units per portion	Size of average portion
bolognese	40	240	¼	I	6 oz (171 g)
bread	30	60	¾	I½	2 oz (57 g)
brown, bottled	30	30	I½	I½	I oz (30 g)
cheese	55	220	½	2	4 oz (114 g)
ketchup	30	30	I	I	I oz (30 g)
onion	30	60	½	I	2 oz (57 g)
tomato	25	100	½	2	4 oz (114 g)
white, savoury	40	160	½	2	4 oz (114 g)
white, sweet	50	200	I	4	4 oz (114 g)
sauerkraut, canned	5	20	¼	I	4 oz (114 g)
sausages					
beef, fried	75	150	½	I	I sausage
beef, grilled	55	110	½	I	I sausage
pork, fried	90	180	¾	I	I sausage
pork, grilled	90	125	¾	I	I sausage
liver	90	90	¼	¼	I oz (30 g)
sausage roll					
flaky pastry	135	270	2	4	I small
short pastry	110	220	2	4	I small
saveloy	75	150	½	I	2 oz (57 g)
savouries					
cheese straws	160	160	I½	I½	I oz (30 g)
twiglets	100	5	8	½	I twiglet
potato rings	150	150	3½	3½	I oz (30 g)
scallops					
raw	30	30	0	0	I oz (30 g)

	Calories per 1 oz (30 g)	Calories per portion	Carbohydrate units per 1 oz (30 g)	Carbohydrate units per portion	Size of average portion
steamed	30	90	0	0	2 fish
fried	35	115	0	0	2 fish
canned	30	90	0	0	3 oz (85 g)
scampi					
boiled	30	120	0	0	3 pieces
fried in batter	55	275	½	2	3 pieces
fried in breadcrumbs	90	450	2	8	3 pieces
schnapps	65	65	3	3	1 oz (30 ml)
screw driver	45	220	2	10	¼ pt (142 ml)
scones					
plain	85	130	2½	4	1 medium
cheese	100	200	2½	4½	1 medium
currant	105	160	3½	5	1 medium
scotch egg	275	550	¾	4	1 egg
scotch pancakes	80	120	2	3	1 medium
seakale, boiled	2	10	0	0	5 oz (142 g)
semi-skimmed milk	15	15	¼	¼	1 oz (30 ml)
semi sweet biscuit	130	50	4½	1½	1 biscuit
semolina					
raw	100	100	4	4	1 oz (30 g)
pudding	35	220	1	6	6 oz (171 g)
shandy	10	80	¾	4	½ pt (284 ml)
shepherd's pie	35	350	½	5	10 oz (284 g)
sherry					
dry	35	70	1½	3	2 oz (57 ml)

	Calories per 1 oz (30 g)	Calories per portion	Carbohydrate units per 1 oz (30 g)	Carbohydrate units per portion	Size of average portion
medium	35	70	1¾	3½	2 oz (57 ml)
sweet	40	80	2	4	2 oz (57 ml)
shortbread	145	95	3½	2½	1 biscuit
shortcrust pastry					
raw	130	130	2½	2½	1 oz (30 g)
cooked	150	150	3	3	1 oz (30 g)
shredded wheat	90	90	4	4	1 oz (30 g)
shrimps					
raw in shells	10	10	0	0	1 oz (30 g)
raw, shelled	30	60	0	0	2 oz (57 g)
boiled	30	60	0	0	2 oz (57 g)
potted	120	240	0	0	2 oz (57 g)
simnel cake	110	440	3	12	4 oz (114 g)
skate					
raw	20	20	0	0	1 oz (30 g)
steamed	25	130	0	0	5 oz (142 g)
fried in batter	35	170	½	3	6 oz (171 g)
fried in breadcrumbs	50	300	¼	1	6 oz (171 g)
skimmed milk					
fresh	10	10	¼	¼	1 oz (30 ml)
dried	100	15	3	½	2 tsp
snails with butter	180	270	0	0	6 snails
soda bread	60	60	1	1	1 oz (30 g)
soda water	0	0	0	0	4 oz (114 ml)
sole, lemon or Dover					
raw	25	25	0	0	1 oz (30 g)

	Calories per 1 oz (30 g)	Calories per portion	Carbohydrate units per 1 oz (30 g)	Carbohydrate units per portion	Size of average portion
steamed	25	130	0	0	5 oz (142 g)
fried in breadcrumbs	60	310	0	½	5 oz (142 g)

SOUP

chicken cream	15	140	0	2	½ pt (284 ml)
chicken noodle	5	55	0	2	½ pt (284 ml)
consommé	10	70	0	0	½ pt (284 ml)
French onion	30	270	½	4	½ pt (284 ml)
lentil	30	300	¾	6	½ pt (284 ml)
minestrone	5	65	¼	2	½ pt (284 ml)
mulligatawny	10	100	½	3	½ pt (284 ml)
mushroom	15	150	¼	2	½ pt (284 ml)
oxtail	15	150	0	2	½ pt (284 ml)
tomato	15	150	¼	3	½ pt (284 ml)
vegetable	10	100	¼	4	½ pt (284 ml)
soured cream	55	55	0	0	1 oz (30 ml)
soya bean					
raw	115	115	2	2	1 oz (30 g)
cooked	10	40	¼	1	4 oz (114 g)
soya flour					
full fat	130	130	1½	1½	1 oz (30 g)
low fat	100	100	2	2	1 oz (30 g)
soya oil	255	255	0	0	1 oz (30 ml)
spaghetti					
raw	105	105	5	5	1 oz (30 g)

	Calories per 1 oz (30 g)	Calories per portion	Carbohydrate units per 1 oz (30 g)	Carbohydrate units per portion	Size of average portion
boiled	35	200	1½	9	6 oz (171 g)
in tomato sauce	15	100	¾	4	6 oz (171 g)
spinach raw	10	10	0	0	1 oz (30 g)
boiled	10	50	0	0	6 oz (171 g)
sponge biscuit, chocolate covered	150	50	6	2	1 biscuit
sponge cake with fat	130	260	3	6	2 oz (57 g)
fatless	85	170	3	6	2 oz (57 g)
with jam	85	170	3½	7	2 oz (57 g)
sponge pudding	100	400	2½	10	4 oz (114 g)
sprats raw	25	25	0	0	1 oz (30 g)
fried	125	500	0	0	4 oz (114 g)
fried in batter	125	500	½	2	4 oz (114 g)
spring greens raw	10	10	0	0	1 oz (30 g)
boiled	10	40	0	0	4 oz (114 g)
sprouts, Brussels raw	10	10	0	0	1 oz (30 g)
boiled	5	30	0	0	6 oz (171 g)
squash, lemon or orange, undiluted	30	30	1½	1½	1 oz (30 ml)
squid raw	20	20	0	0	1 oz (30 g)

	Calories per 1 oz (30 g)	Calories per portion	Carbohydrate units per 1 oz (30 g)	Carbohydrate units per portion	Size of average portion
steamed	25	125	0	0	5 oz (142 g)
fried	35	170	0	0	5 oz (142 g)
starch reduced crispbread	110	30	2	½	1 biscuit
starch reduced roll	110	25	2½	½	1 roll
steak & kidney pie single crust	80	640	1	8	8 oz (227 g)
individual	90	735	1½	11	8 oz (227 g)
sterilized milk	20	20	¼	¼	1 oz (30 ml)
stew, beef	35	340	¼	2	10 oz (284 g)
stew, Irish	35	530	½	9	15 oz (426 g)
stewed steak with gravy	50	400	0	0	8 oz (227 g)
stilton cheese	130	130	0	0	1 oz (30 g)
stout, bottled	10	100	½	5½	½ pt (284 ml)
strawberries raw	10	45	¼	2	6 oz (171 g)
canned	25	125	1	5	5 oz (142 g)
strawberry mousse, frozen	40	110	1	2½	3½ oz (100 g)
strong ale	20	200	1	10	½ pt (284 ml)
suet block	255	255	0	0	1 oz (30 g)
shredded	235	235	¾	¾	1 oz (30 g)
suet pudding, steamed	95	475	2	11	5 oz (142 g)

	Calories per 1 oz (30 g)	Calories per portion	Carbohydrate units per 1 oz (30 g)	Carbohydrate units per portion	Size of average portion
sugar, white or brown	110	20	6	1	1 tsp
sugar-coated puffed wheat	100	100	5	5	1 oz (30 g)
sultanas, dried	70	70	3½	3½	1 oz (30 g)
sultana cake	100	300	3	9	3 oz (85 g)
sunflower oil	255	255	0	0	1 oz (30 ml)
swedes raw	5	5	0	0	1 oz (30 g)
boiled	5	30	¼	1	6 oz (171 g)
sweetbread lamb, raw	35	35	0	0	1 oz (30 g)
lamb, fried	65	260	¼	1	4 oz (114 g)
sweetcorn on cob, boiled	35	175	1	6	1 medium
canned	20	80	1	4	4 oz (114 g)
sweet potatoes raw	25	25	1	1	1 oz (30 g)
boiled	25	100	1	4	4 oz (114 g)
sweets, boiled	95	95	5	5	1 oz (30 g)

SWEETS AND CHOCOLATES

after dinner mints	120	120	4	4	1 oz (30 g)
boiled sweets e.g. fruit drops, clear mints	95	95	5	5	1 oz (30 g)

	Calories per 1 oz (30 g)	Calories per portion	Carbohydrate units per 1 oz (30 g)	Carbohydrate units per portion	Size of average portion
chocolate egg, cream filled	45	170	3½	6	1 egg
fruit gums	50	50	2½	2½	1 oz (30 g)
fruit pastilles	70	70	3½	3½	1 oz (30 g)
fudge	130	130	4½	4½	1 oz (30 g)
jelly babies	100	100	5	5	1 oz (30 g)
liquorice gums	70	70	3½	3½	1 oz (30 g)
all sorts	90	90	4	4	1 oz (30 g)
sticks	85	85	4	4	1 oz (30 g)
marzipan	125	125	3	3	1 oz (30 g)
marshmallows	95	95	4½	4½	1 oz (30 g)
milk chocolate	150	150	3½	3½	1 oz (30 g)
+ brazil nuts	155	155	2½	2½	1 oz (30 g)
+ fruit & nuts	140	140	3	3	1 oz (30 g)
+ wholenut	165	165	3	3	1 oz (30 g)
milk chocolate caramel bar	135	270	3	5½	2 oz (57 g) bar
caramel & fudge	135	270	4	7½	2 oz (57 g) bar
caramel & nuts	150	225	3½	5½	1½ oz (43 g) bar
coconut bar	140	140	3	3	1 oz (30 g)
fudge	125	125	3½	3½	1 finger
wafer biscuit	145	110	3½	2½	2 wafers
peppermints	110	110	6	6	1 oz (30 g)
peppermint creams	100	100	5½	5½	1 oz (30 g)

	Calories per 1 oz (30 g)	Calories per portion	Carbohydrate units per 1 oz (30 g)	Carbohydrate units per portion	Size of average portion
plain chocolate covered	120	120	4	4	1 oz (30 g)
plain chocolate	150	150	3½	3½	1 oz (30 g)
+ almonds	160	160	3	3	1 oz (30 g)
covered peppermint cream bar	130	130	4	4	1 oz (30 g) bar
toffees assorted	120	120	4	4	1 oz (30 g)
chocolate coated, assorted	130	130	3½	3½	1 oz (30 g)
Swiss roll	75	290	3	12	4 oz (114 g)
syrup, golden	85	85	4½	4½	1 tbsp

	Calories per 1 oz (30 g)	Calories per portion	Carbohydrate units per 1 oz (30 g)	Carbohydrate units per portion	Size of average portion
tagliatelle raw	105	105	5	5	1 oz (30 g)
boiled	35	200	1½	9	6 oz (171 g)

	Calories per 1 oz (30 g)	Calories per portion	Carbohydrate units per 1 oz (30 g)	Carbohydrate units per portion	Size of average portion
tangerine	5	20	¼	1	1 medium
canned	15	60	1	3	4 oz (114 g)
tapioca					
raw	100	100	5	5	1 oz (30 g)
pudding	35	220	1	4	4 oz (114 g)
taramasalata	90	180	½	1	2 oz (57 g)
tart, custard	95	370	2	7	4 oz (114 g)
tart, jam	120	120	3½	3½	1 tart
tartare sauce	140	140	0	0	1 oz (30 g)
teacake	85	170	3	6	1 teacake
Tia Maria	90	90	3	3	1 oz (30 ml)
toast, white	85	85	3½	3½	1 oz (30 g)
toffees, mixed	120	120	4	4	1 oz (30 g)
Tom Collins	25	250	¾	8	½ pt (284 ml)
tomatoes					
raw	4	15	0	0	1 medium
fried	20	80	0	0	1 medium
chutney	45	45	2	2	1 oz (30 g)
juice	4	20	0	1	¼ pt (142 ml)
ketchup	30	30	1	1	1 oz (30 g)
purée	20	20	¾	¾	1 oz (30 g)
sauce	25	100	½	2	4 oz (114 g)
soup, canned	15	150	¼	3	½ pt (284 ml)
tomé au raisin	80	80	0	0	1 oz (30 g)
tongue					
lamb, raw	55	55	0	0	1 oz (30 g)

	Calories per 1 oz (30 g)	Calories per portion	Carbohydrate units per 1 oz (30 g)	Carbohydrate units per portion	Size of average portion
sheep, stewed	80	490	0	0	6 oz (171 g)
ox, pickled	60	60	0	0	1 oz (30 g)
ox, boiled	85	170	0	0	2 oz (57 g)
canned	60	120	0	0	2 oz (57 g)
tonic water	5	20	¼	1	4 oz (114 ml)
treacle, black	75	35	4	2	1 tbsp
treacle tart	105	420	3½	14	4 oz (114 g)
trifle	45	370	1	7	6 oz (171 g)
tripe					
dressed	15	15	0	0	1 oz (30 g)
stewed	30	180	0	0	6 oz (171 g)
trout					
raw	25	25	0	0	1 oz (30 g)
steamed	25	200	0	0	1 small
fried	40	320	0	0	1 small
smoked	25	200	0	0	1 small
tuna canned in oil, drained	80	160	0	0	1 small can
turbot					
raw	20	20	0	0	1 oz (30 g)
steamed	30	140	0	0	5 oz (142 g)
fried in breadcrumbs	50	250	¼	1	5 oz (142 g)
turkey					
raw, meat only	30	30	0	0	1 oz (30 g)
raw, meat & skin	40	40	0	0	1 oz (30 g)
roast, meat only	40	160	0	0	4 oz (114 g)

	Calories per 1 oz (30 g)	Calories per portion	Carbohydrate units per 1 oz (30 g)	Carbohydrate units per portion	Size of average portion
meat & skin	50	200	0	0	4 oz (114 g)
light meat	35	150	0	0	4 oz (114 g)
dark meat	40	170	0	0	4 oz (114 g)
turnips raw	5	5	0	0	1 oz (30 g)
boiled	4	25	0	¾	6 oz (171 g)
turnip tops, boiled	3	20	0	0	6 oz (171 g)

veal cutlet fried	60	365	¼	1½	1 cutlet
fillet raw	30	30	0	0	1 oz (30 g)
roast	65	260	0	0	4 oz (114 g)
jellied	35	140	0	0	4 oz (114 g)

	Calories per 1 oz (30 g)	Calories per portion	Carbohydrate units per 1 oz (30 g)	Carbohydrate units per portion	Size of average portion
VEGETABLES					
ackee, canned	45	180	0	0	4 oz (114 g)
artichokes					
globe, boiled	5	10	¼	½	1 medium
heart, boiled	4	15	0	½	4 oz (114 g)
heart, canned	4	15	0	½	4 oz (114 g)
Jerusalem, boiled	5	20	¼	1	4 oz (114 g)
asparagus					
boiled	5	20	0	¼	4 oz (114 g)
canned	3	10	0	¼	4 oz (114 g)
aubergine					
fried	35	140	¼	1	4 oz (114 g)
baked	25	100	¼	1	4 oz (114 g)
avocado pear	65	250	0	½	½ large
bamboo shoots, canned	10	10	¼	¼	1 oz (30 g)
beans					
French boiled	2	10	0	0	5 oz (142 g)
runner, boiled	5	20	0	0	4 oz (114 g)
baked	20	100	½	3	5 oz (142 g)
broad, boiled	15	60	½	2	4 oz (114 g)
butter, boiled	25	100	1	4	4 oz (114 g)
haricot, boiled	25	100	1	4	4 oz (114 g)
mung, raw	65	65	2	2	1 oz (30 g)
mung, cooked	30	60	¾	1½	2 oz (57 g)
red kidney, cooked	25	100	1	4	4 oz (114 g)

	Calories per 1 oz (30 g)	Calories per portion	Carbohydrate units per 1 oz (30 g)	Carbohydrate units per portion	Size of average portion
soya, raw	115	115	2	2	1 oz (30 g)
soya, cooked	10	40	¼	1	4 oz (114 g)
beansprouts raw or boiled	3	15	0	0	5 oz (142 g)
canned	5	25	0	0	5 oz (142 g)
beetroot, boiled	15	30	½	1	2 oz (57 g)
broccoli tops, boiled	5	20	0	0	4 oz (114 g)
Brussels sprouts, boiled	5	30	0	0	6 oz (171 g)
cabbage red, raw	5	20	0	0	3 oz (85 g)
red, boiled	4	15	0	0	4 oz (114 g)
red, pickled	5	5	0	0	1 oz (30 g)
savoy, boiled	3	10	0	0	4 oz (114 g)
white, raw	3	10	0	0	4 oz (114 g)
white, boiled	4	15	0	0	4 oz (114 g)
capers	0	0	0	0	1 oz (30 g)
carrots old, raw or boiled	5	20	¼	1	4 oz (114 g)
young, raw	5	30	½	1	4 oz (114 g)
young, boiled	4	15	¼	1	4 oz (114 g)
young, canned	5	20	¼	1	4 oz (114 g)
juice	5	25	½	2	¼ pt (142 ml)
cauliflower raw	4	15	0	0	4 oz (114 g)
boiled	3	10	0	0	4 oz (114 g)
pickled	3	3	0	0	1 oz (30 g)

	Calories per 1 oz (30 g)	Calories per portion	Carbohydrate units per 1 oz (30 g)	Carbohydrate units per portion	Size of average portion
celeriac					
raw	5	10	0	0	2 oz (57 g)
boiled	4	15	0	0	4 oz (114 g)
celery					
raw	2	5	0	0	2 oz (57 g)
boiled	2	5	0	0	2 oz (57 g)
canned	1	5	0	0	4 oz (114 g)
chicory					
raw	3	5	0	0	2 oz (57 g)
boiled	3	10	0	0	4 oz (114 g)
corn on cob, boiled	35	175	1	6	1 medium
courgette					
raw	3	3	0	0	1 oz (30 g)
boiled	1	5	0	¼	4 oz (114 g)
fried	35	140	0	½	4 oz (114 g)
cucumber					
raw	3	3	0	0	1 oz (30 g)
pickled	3	3	¼	¼	1 oz (30 g)
endive					
raw	3	5	0	0	2 oz (57 g)
boiled	3	10	0	0	4 oz (114 g)
garlic	5	1	0	0	1 clove
horseradish, raw	15	15	½	½	1 oz (30 g)
laverbread	15	15	0	0	1 oz (30 g)
leeks					
raw	10	10	0	0	1 oz (30 g)

	Calories per 1 oz (30 g)	Calories per portion	Carbohydrate units per 1 oz (30 g)	Carbohydrate units per portion	Size of average portion
boiled	5	30	0	0	4 oz (114 g)
lentils					
raw	85	85	3	3	1 oz (30 g)
split boiled	30	120	1	4	4 oz (114 g)
lettuce, raw	3	10	0	0	3 oz (85 g)
marrow					
raw	3	3	0	0	1 oz (30 g)
boiled	1	5	0	0	4 oz (114 g)
mushrooms					
raw	4	4	0	0	1 oz (30 g)
boiled	2	5	0	0	2 oz (57 g)
fried	60	120	0	0	2 oz (57 g)
okra					
raw	5	5	0	0	1 oz (30 g)
boiled or canned	5	20	0	0	4 oz (114 g)
olives					
black or green	25	25	0	0	10 olives
stuffed	30	30	0	0	10 olives
onions					
raw	5	5	0	0	1 oz (30 g)
boiled	4	15	0	0	4 oz (114 g)
fried	100	100	½	½	1 oz (30 g)
parsley, raw	5	5	0	0	1 oz (30 g)
parsnips, boiled	15	60	¾	3	4 oz (114 g)
peas					
fresh raw	20	20	½	½	1 oz (30 g)

	Calories per 1 oz (30 g)	Calories per portion	Carbohydrate units per 1 oz (30 g)	Carbohydrate units per portion	Size of average portion
boiled	15	45	½	1	3 oz (85 g)
frozen, raw	15	15	½	½	1 oz (30 g)
boiled	10	30	¼	1	3 oz (85 g)
canned, garden	15	45	½	1	3 oz (85 g)
canned, processed	25	65	¾	3	3 oz (85 g)
dried, raw	80	80	3	3	1 oz (30 g)
dried, boiled	30	90	1	3	3 oz (85 g)
split, raw	90	90	3	3	1 oz (30 g)
split, boiled	35	105	1	4	3 oz (85 g)
chick, raw	90	90	3	3	1 oz (30 g)
chick, boiled	40	160	1	4	4 oz (114 g)
red pigeon, raw	85	85	3	3	1 oz (30 g)
red pigeon, cooked	30	90	1	3	3 oz (85 g)
peppers					
raw	4	10	0	0	2 oz (57 g)
boiled	4	10	0	0	2 oz (57 g)
plantain green					
boiled	35	140	2	7	4 oz (114 g)
ripe, fried	75	300	2½	7	4 oz (114 g)
potatoes					
old, boiled	25	100	1	4	4 oz (114 g)
old, mashed	35	140	1	4	4 oz (114 g)
old, baked	30	120	1½	6	1 small
old, roast	45	180	1½	6	2 small
chips, fresh	70	430	2	12	6 oz (171 g)
chips, frozen	30	30	1	1	1 oz (30 g)

	Calories per 1 oz (30 g)	Calories per portion	Carbohydrate units per 1 oz (30 g)	Carbohydrate units per portion	Size of average portion
chips, fried	80	495	2	10	6 oz (171 g)
new, boiled	20	85	1	4	4 oz (114 g)
instant, powder	90	90	4	4	1 oz (30 g)
instant, made up	20	80	1	4	4 oz (114 g)
crisps	150	125	3	2½	small pkt
pumpkin raw	4	4	0	0	1 oz (30 g)
boiled	2	10	0	0	5 oz (142 g)
radishes, raw	4	4	0	0	1 oz (30 g)
salsify raw	5	5	0	0	1 oz (30 g)
boiled	5	20	0	0	4 oz (114 g)
sauerkraut, canned	5	20	¼	1	4 oz (114 g)
seakale, boiled	2	10	0	0	5 oz (142 g)
spinach raw	10	10	0	0	1 oz (30 g)
boiled	10	50	0	0	6 oz (171 g)
spring greens raw	10	10	0	0	1 oz (30 g)
boiled	10	40	0	0	4 oz (114 g)
swedes raw	5	5	0	0	1 oz (30 g)
boiled	5	30	¼	1	6 oz (171 g)
sweet corn, canned	20	80	1	4	4 oz (114 g)
sweet potatoes raw	25	25	1	1	1 oz (30 g)

	Calories per 1 oz (30 g)	Calories per portion	Carbohydrate units per 1 oz (30 g)	Carbohydrate units per portion	Size of average portion
boiled	25	100	1	4	4 oz (114 g)
tomatoes					
raw	4	15	0	0	1 medium
fried	20	80	0	0	1 medium
juice	4	20	0	1	¼ pt (142 ml)
turnips					
raw	5	5	0	0	1 oz (30 g)
boiled	4	25	0	¾	6 oz (171 g)
turnip tops, boiled	3	20	0	0	6 oz (171 g)
watercress, raw	4	4	0	0	1 oz (30 g)
yam					
raw	35	35	2	2	1 oz (30 g)
boiled	35	205	2	10	6 oz (171 g)
vegetable oils	255	255	0	0	1 oz (30 ml)
vegetable soup	10	100	¼	4	½ pt (284 ml)
venison					
raw	40	40	0	0	1 oz (30 g)
roast	55	220	0	0	4 oz (114 g)
fried	65	250	0	0	4 oz (114 g)
grilled	55	225	0	0	4 oz (114 g)
vermouth					
dry	35	70	2	4	2 oz (57 ml)
sweet	45	90	2½	5	2 oz (57 ml)
vodka	65	65	3	3	1 oz (30 ml)
vodka cocktail	50	160	2	6	3 oz (85 ml)

	Calories per 1 oz (30 g)	Calories per portion	Carbohydrate units per 1 oz (30 g)	Carbohydrate units per portion	Size of average portion
wafers	75	10	15	3	1 wafer
wafer biscuit, filled	150	70	4	1½	1 wafer
walnuts, shelled	150	150	¼	¼	1 oz (30 g)
water biscuit	125	60	4½	2	1 biscuit
watercress	4	4	0	0	1 oz (30 g)
watermelon	5	50	¼	3	large slice
Welsh rarebit	105	420	1	4½	4 oz (114 g)
wensleydale cheese	110	110	0	0	1 oz (30 g)
wheatgerm	100	50	3	1½	½ oz (14 g)
whelks boiled in shells	4	4	0	0	1 oz (30 g)
shelled	25	75	0	0	3 oz (85 g)
whisky	65	65	3	3	1 oz (30 ml)
whisky sour	55	240	2½	11	4½ oz (128 ml)
whitebait raw	15	15	0	0	1 oz (30 g)

	Calories per 1 oz (30 g)	Calories per portion	Carbohydrate units per 1 oz (30 g)	Carbohydrate units per portion	Size of average portion
fried in batter	150	590	½	2	4 oz (114 g)
fried in flour	150	590	¼	1	4 oz (114 g)
white currants					
raw	5	30	¼	1	4 oz (114 g)
stewed, no sugar	5	25	¼	1	4 oz (114 g)
stewed + sugar	15	60	1	3	4 oz (114 g)
white pudding	130	255	2	4	2 oz (57 g)
white sauce					
savoury	40	160	½	2	4 oz (114 g)
sweet	50	200	1	4	4 oz (114 g)
whiting					
fried	55	275	½	2	5 oz (142 g)
steamed	25	130	0	0	5 oz (142 g)
wholemeal bread	60	60	2½	2½	1 oz (30 g)
wholemeal flour	90	90	3½	3½	1 oz (30 g)
wine					
red	20	100	1	5	¼ pt (142 ml)
rosé	20	100	1	5	¼ pt (142 ml)
white, dry	20	100	1	5	¼ pt (142 ml)
white, medium	20	100	1	5	¼ pt (142 ml)
white, sweet	25	125	1½	7	¼ pt (142 ml)
white, sparkling	20	100	1	5	¼ pt (142 ml)
winkles					
boiled in shell	4	4	0	0	1 oz (30 g)
shelled	20	60	0	0	3 oz (85 g)
woodcock, roast	20	160	0	0	1 bird

126

	Calories per 1 oz (30 g)	Calories per portion	Carbohydrate units per 1 oz (30 g)	Carbohydrate units per portion	Size of average portion
yam, boiled	35	205	2	10	6 oz (171 g)
yeast					
fresh	15	15	0	0	1 oz (30 g)
dried	50	50	0	0	1 oz (30 g)
yeast extract	50	5	0	0	½ tsp
yogurt, low fat					
natural	15	75	¼	1	small carton
sweetened	25	130	1	4½	small carton
flavoured	25	125	¾	4	small carton
fruit	30	135	1	5	small carton
hazelnut	30	150	1	5	small carton
yorkshire pudding	60	120	1½	3	1 small